Books by Laura Bradbury

The Winemakers Trilogy
A Vineyard for Two
Love in the Vineyards

Grape Series
My Grape Year
My Grape Québec
My Grape Paris
My Grape Wedding
My Grape Escape
My Grape Village
My Grape Cellar

Other Writings:
Philosophy of Preschoolers

Laura Bradbury and Rebecca Wellman
Bisous & Brioche

my grape christmas

my grape Christmas

LAURA BRADBURY

Published by Grape Books

Print Edition

Paperback ISBN: 978-1-989784-12-9
eBook ISBN: 978-1-989784-11-2

Visit: www.laurabradbury.com

This one is a 2020 holiday gift for all my awesome readers who have helped me get through this craptastic year. I love you all, and here's for a better and brighter 2021 for all of us. In the meantime, get cozy, pour yourself a glass of something nice, and escape for a few hours with me.

"C'est Noel: Il est grand temps de rallumer les étoiles"
—Guillaume Apollinaire

chapter one

The wind whistling down the rue Saint Laurent felt like it was blowing directly from the North Pole. I felt its frigid force reverberate out from my torso as I shuffled along. The sidewalk was a sheet of ice and had been for the past three weeks, so I hunched over into that half-skating, half-walking gait that everyone adopted when Montréal was in the grip of winter.

The glacial temperatures came early this year, according to the locals. Usually the city didn't plunge into its months-long deep freeze until January, but this year it had hit in early December, so I was finding that Christmas shopping felt more like an expedition to the polar icecap.

The bags hanging off my arm were cutting into me. I wished I could go back to our apartment, but I didn't relish the idea of confronting our unhinged roommate alone. Franck would be back from work in about an hour, so I would just have to wait until then.

The familiar sign of our favorite food shop, *La Vieille Europe*, appeared in front of me. It was a miracle I could see anything at all, as I was squinting to protect my poor eyeballs from the icy snow being driven against my face.

I burst into the shop. *No snow. No wind. Ahhhhhh.* I dropped my bags to the floor and took a deep breath of the warm air. It smelled of cured sausages, ripe cheeses, and strong espresso. *Heaven.* I was half-way through a deep sigh of relief when I was shoved from the back.

"*Excusez-moi Mademoiselle, mais—*"

"*Désolé*," I mumbled and scrambled out of his way. Of all the wise places to take a rest, in front of the door of my favorite food shop probably wasn't one of them.

My feet needed to thaw, and a trickle of melting snow was dripping down the nape of my neck. An espresso break was in order. There was no room for tables in the crowded, bustling shop, so the espresso was served at a long, bar height wooden counter as it was in many French cafés.

When Franck first arrived, the two of us would dream of *La Vieille Europe* espresso, but we could barely afford to buy rye bread and cans of tuna. Now that Franck was working a steady job for a survey company, and both he and I had saved up money all summer—Franck as a deckhand on a fishing boat up near the Alaskan border, and me as a Customs Officer in Victoria—we could afford the occasional espresso. Man, did we ever appreciate it, like I did right now.

At the counter it was me and a cluster of garrulous Italian men. If I hadn't spent a year in France, I probably would have thought they were arguing, but now I knew better. They were talking, and friendly conversation in the latin countries of Europe, like France, involved strenuous debate and raised voices. It was all in good fun, so to speak.

I shoved all my bags under the counter and unzipped my puffy winter jacket. Inside *La Vieille Europe* it was always boiling. I was already sweating underneath my layers of clothes and I knew from experience that sweat would flash-freeze on my skin the moment I stepped outside again. Sweating. Freezing. Sweating. Freezing. That was Montréal in the winter.

The espresso was quickly served to me in a tiny ceramic cup with "Illy" emblazoned on the side—the name of a well-known Italian espresso company that I'd seen used in bars and cafés all over France.

I breathed in the delicious steam rising from my cup and unwrapped a sugar cube from the round metal dispenser that looked like a pac-man. I dropped it in with a plop and stirred it slowly.

The espresso was a consolation, at least, for not being able to return home right away. The previous year—Franck's first in Montréal and our first year living together—we'd been instructed by the police to leave our first apartment in the middle of the night. It turned out our dodgy landlord who'd been making threatening phone calls to us was in the mafia and had a criminal record as long as my arm. Thank God we'd managed to find a new place at that time of night.

This year, we'd decided to take on a roommate and share an apartment. Everyone did that in Montréal, and through a friend of a friend we'd been put in contact with a girl from Toronto who was looking for someone to share the rent.

Neither Franck nor I would have considered taking on a roommate if our budget wasn't so small, or the fact that us living with a roommate was, for some illogical reason, slightly more palatable to my parents than just Franck and me living together.

Besides, I'd seen the previous year that with the help of roommates it was possible to get bigger and better apartments than we could if it was just the two of us. Also, I was worried about becoming too insulated in our couple bubble and a roommate was a built-in social life. It could only be good, right?

The Toronto girl's name was Ava, and we were thrilled when she offered to come to Montréal early and find an apartment for the three of us.

The location was good, at the top of Coloniale Avenue near Saint Laurent and the Plateau, but far enough away from our old mafia landlord that we didn't feel as though we needed to sleep with one eye open.

When we arrived From British Columbia at the very end of August and met Ava, she seemed fantastic.

Sure, she'd given us the smaller of the two bedrooms, even though we were sharing one and she was alone, but she'd done the legwork to find the place, so that was fair. Then, she announced she'd only be paying a third of the rent and that we needed to cover the other two thirds, even though we only took up one bedroom. We shrugged. It was true, we reasoned, that we used up heat and hot water for two people, so we'd just accept it...

Then Ava started to go days without speaking to us and muttering unintelligible but ominous sounding things under her breath.

Her boyfriend dumped her, and instead of getting over him like we tried to help her do, she was getting stranger by the day. Franck and I were counting down the days until we left for Christmas break.

That was why I was so intent on finding the perfect presents. For Christmas, rather than returning to my family on the West Coast like we'd done the year before, we were heading back to Burgundy. It would be Franck's first time back home since he'd left his life in France to come and be with me in Québec.

The trip would also be my first time back to Burgundy since I'd left it after my exchange year—the year everything in my life changed—ended. I remembered Franck's father, André, taking us to the train station to catch our train to Paris so I could catch my flight back to Canada. I didn't know if I'd ever see Burgundy again. At that point, I didn't know if I'd even see Franck again.

I was excited and nervous, and if my mother had taught me anything in life, it was that I shouldn't arrive empty-handed. There had to be lots of presents—*thoughtful* presents—for Franck's family. That's what filled my shopping bags.

I'd found the perfect thing for everyone on my list—no small task, as Franck's family was large and far-reaching. The only one who I didn't have something for was Franck's quiet father. I'd have to find something over the next two days, as that's when we were scheduled to catch an Air France plane to Paris out of the Mirabel airport.

The last time I'd been there was when Franck arrived in Montréal for the first time so that we could be together. So much had happened since then. We'd changed, both separately and as a couple. Had the same thing have happened with Franck's friends and family in France? More importantly, how would I be welcomed considering I was the girl who had taken their beloved Franck away from them?

Thank God I had the presents. They were my peace offering.

I found myself at the front door of our apartment at the exact same time as Franck. I could hear a "*salut, toi!*" laugh coming from behind the layers of scarf he'd wrapped around his neck and mouth.

He grabbed as many of my bags as he could hold and unlocked the door for both of us. We stamped the snow off our boots in the front hallway.

Maybe things didn't feel friendly anymore with Ava, but that didn't mean I had to acknowledge the palpable tension in the apartment. I'd been taught by my W.A.S.P. upbringing that pleasantness can steamroll over most conflicts.

"Hello Ava!" I called out. "We're home."

There were a few seconds of silence, during which I began to hope for a few gleeful moments that perhaps Franck and I were alone in the apartment.

"Why should I care?" Ava's words echoed down the long hallway. My eyes met Franck's. He'd pulled off enough of his scarf that I saw his grimace.

He shook his head. "I don't know why you bother."

"To keep it civil."

Frank shrugged. "So she doesn't talk to us? So what? It's quieter that way. Don't let it bother you."

"I can't *not* let it bother me," I said, going into our bedroom and hoping Franck would follow. I truly didn't feel comfortable having this conversation in the hall where Ava could probably hear everything. "I was brought up to avoid conflict."

"Ugh." Franck shut our bedroom door behind him. "That sounds tedious."

"It is," I said. "But I just can't shake it. It's part of being Canadian."

"Ava's Canadian," Franck pointed out. "Yet avoiding conflict doesn't seem to be high on her priority list."

"I know." I threw my shopping bags down on the bed. "It's

like she missed the memo from her fellow Canadians."

Franck's eyes grew round. "What's in all those bags?"

"Presents for everyone in France." I plopped down on the bed and began taking things out of the bags to organize them.

Franck threw off his coat and leapt on top of me on the bed. "I had other plans for you and this bed, *tu sais*."

I shrieked and tried to push his solid weight off me. "Some of these are fragile! We're going to break them."

Franck kissed my neck ravenously. His lips were deliciously warm and his hair smelled of snow and our vanilla shampoo. "Don't care," floated up, muffled by my hair.

I lay back and pretended to give up. "Do your worst, just don't blame me when your family opens up a bunch of broken stuff on Christmas morning."

I felt rather than heard Franck sigh against me and the fight went out of him. "You're right." He sat up. "But do we really need all this?"

I knew that Christmas in France wasn't as focused on presents as it was at my family's home on the West Coast of Canada. From what I'd seen, the food and wine aspects of the celebrations were considered far more important than gifts. "I'm not walking into your house empty-handed."

"Why not? It wouldn't matter. My family loves you."

I cocked a brow. "Maybe so, but I *have* taken their son away from them for over a year."

Franck pursed his lips. "Maybe the presents are not such a bad idea after all."

"Just so."

A series of rapid knocks on the door made both our heads swivel. "Ava?" I wondered out loud, a lead ball of dread in my gut as I wondered what she was going to spring on us this time.

"It has to be," Franck whispered. "You answer. She hates me more than she hates you."

"How do you figure that?"

He shrugged. "Unlike me, you still make an effort to remain civil."

He certainly had a point there. Franck was well-versed in the silent treatment his family all gave each other on a regular basis, so he felt no such compunction.

"Fine," I muttered. "But I might need back-up."

"I'll be here," he said, starting to pull things out of my bags to look at them.

I opened the door. There was Ava, her eyes wild and her red hair sticking out all over the place. Her eyes were bloodshot and shiny. I had no idea what was going on with her, but my compassion was stirred all the same. She looked wretched.

"Are you okay?" I asked, keeping my voice as gentle as possible.

"Don't you start!" She put her hands on her hips and glared at me.

Okay then. "Start what?"

"I've had a difficult enough day without you guys sitting in your bedroom laughing at me."

"We weren't laughing at you." At least not *entirely*. "I bought a bunch of presents to take to France for Franck's family. We were talking about those."

"Well, isn't that lovely for you two," she said. "You make me *sick*."

My empathy was replaced by annoyance. "Look Ava, I'm sorry if you're going through a rough time, but that has nothing to do with us."

She crossed her arms and made a *hmph* sound. "Whatever. I just wanted to tell you that if the police come by looking for me, tell them I'm not here."

"What?"

Franck materialized beside me. "Why would the police be looking for you?"

Ava's face went scarlet. "You know my boyfriend dumped me, right?"

I did, but I rather thought acknowledging that would add fuel to her fire. "I noticed he hasn't been around. I'm sorry, but what does that have to do with the police?"

"He has a new girlfriend. She's just *perfect*." Ava raised her voice on that last word to make it mimicking and cruel. "She wears a camel-colored duffel coat and has a golden retriever who matches the color exactly. It makes me want to barf."

That vision kind-of made me nauseous too, but I sensed commiserating with her might backfire. "Oh," I said. "Do you know her?"

"No, but I've been...watching her."

Franck reached out and took my hand behind the partially open door. He squeezed hard. *Good God.* A shiver climbed my spine at the thought of this probably annoying, nameless, camel-coated girl. She probably had no idea she was being stalked by an unhinged ex-girlfriend.

"Like, *stalking* her?" I demanded.

Ava just shrugged. "Today I followed them back to his place and I needed to find out what they were doing inside."

"Why?" Surely, she was just hurting herself.

"I needed to see how they were together in private."

"But—"

"He lives on the second floor, but there's this wooden trellis that goes up to the living room window—"

"You didn't—" But I suspected she did.

"So I started climbing. I lost my shoe about half-way up, but I could hear the TV in his apartment. They were watching Northern Exposure." She spat out these last two words.

"We love that show," I said, then realized after the fact that it probably was not the wisest interjection. Still, even though Franck and I couldn't afford a TV, we did love Northern Exposure when we caught it from time to time somewhere else.

Ava rolled her eyes. "Do you want me to tell you or not?"

Not really, but I waved my hand for her to continue. If the police did show up, it would be advisable to know what to tell them.

"That was always our show. We had dates to watch it together. How dare he be watching it with *her*?" Her eyes flicked to me, but I honestly didn't know what to say. Ava's ex-boyfriend had every right to do what he wanted now they were broken up, and at this juncture I couldn't exactly blame him for dumping her.

"I kept climbing," she continued. "But the thing is the trellis is quite old, and not very well attached to the house, so I was almost at the top and had grabbed hold of the rim of the window then the whole thing fell backwards."

"Oh shit." It must have been humiliating, but hopefully it taught her not to stalk people. "Are you hurt?"

"I hung on to the windowsill as long as I could, but then he opened the window and I fell into a bush below. I scratched my back and sprained my ankle."

I looked down and saw her ankle was banged up in gauze under the leg of her sweatpants. "Did he know it was you?"

She at least had the presence of mind to look ashamed at this...or was it just regret at being caught? "Yeah. He yelled out the window that I was to leave him alone and that he was going to call the police and put a restraining order on me. I half ran, half limped away, but...you know...I guess the police could still come."

"Are you planning on being here to see them if they do?"

She snorted. "As if. I'm going to go back home to Toronto. They won't bother trying to find me there. The thing is I need to catch the bus and I can't really make it down to the bus depot with my ankle and my suitcase."

"How long will you be away for?" I asked.

"I don't know."

"We'll help you down to the depot to make sure you get on the bus, okay?" I was half expecting Franck to give me a little kick in the calf at this offer, but it never came. "When do you want to leave?"

Ava consulted her watch. "Ten minutes."

"We'll be ready," I said. "Meet you in the hall."

"Fine." She walked back down to her room without so much as a thank you.

I shut the door. Franck was still standing close to my side. "Are you as terrified as I am right now?" I asked him.

His olive skin did indeed look paler than usual. "She's completely unhinged," he whispered in a tone that harbingered doom.

I nodded. "Yes, but I figured putting her on that bus gets her out of our hair for a few days until we leave. Besides, she seems desperate."

"You did the right thing." Franck grabbed my coat off the floor and slid it over my right arm, then my left. "We'll send her off safely to her family, then we can concentrate on France."

I nodded. "You're coming with me, right?"

He grabbed his coat off the radiator. "You think I'd let you go alone with her? *Jamais.*"

chapter two

Franck and I walked back along Saint-Laurent from the metro station. We'd helped Ava on her bus and tried to ignore the vitriol that poured out of her mouth concerning her ex and his new paramour. We'd even stayed until the bus pulled out of the berth and waved her on her way.

It was still bitterly cold, so we were hunched over as usual, but with Ava's departure I nevertheless felt like a massive concrete block had been lifted from my shoulders. I hadn't realized just how stressful it was to live with so much unresolved tension in the apartment until her bus had disappeared from sight.

"Do you have to get back to the apartment to study?" Franck asked, peering down at me through the little slit between the bottom of his wool toque and the top of his scarf which was wrapped around his face up to the bridge of his nose.

My only remaining exam was the morning of the day of our flight to Paris. It was for my Survey of Shakespeare course and my professor was as demanding as she was brilliant. Of course I needed to study. When did a second-year university student *not* need to study? Still, needing to study and wanting to study were two entirely different things.

"I do, but I feel so liberated I'm in the mood to celebrate."

Franck squeezed my mitten encased hand with his. "Schwartz's?"

"You read my mind." Despite the icy sidewalk, I almost skipped towards the glowing red sign ahead.

Inside, we were quickly seated against the wall at one of their long communal booths. We didn't have to think at all before ordering now—a smoked meat sandwich on rye and a big fat Kosher pickle for each of us. The spicy smell of pepper and smoke infused the air. I shed my clothing—a procedure I repeated several times over the course of a winter day in Montreal.

"Ahhhhhhhh," Franck sighed as he removed his toque. "This is better." His shoulders dropped by several inches.

"Were your shoulders up around your ears because of Ava the Stalker or because of the cold or because of our trip to France?"

He rubbed his face with his hands. "All of it, I guess."

I blinked. I had thrown the France bit in there for no particular reason. Sure, my excitement about being back in France was infused with nervousness about the reception I would get from Franck's family, but I thought Franck was anticipating our French homecoming with nothing but unmitigated joy. "You're tense about France?" I asked. "I thought it was just me that had… concerns."

Franck shrugged. "I mean, most of all I'm so excited to go back home—to see my family again, and drink kir with Mémé, and hug Emmanuel-Marie, and to eat good cheese, and drink wine—"

"Not sensing a lot of tension so far."

The corner of his mouth quirked up. "I just… I don't know exactly how I'll find things there. I mean, I've been away over a year. We've created a whole different life for ourselves here, one that my family and friends in Burgundy can't even imagine."

"You think?"

"I couldn't truly imagine it until I arrived here."

"Like what exactly?" I nudged his knee with mine under the table. "The delicious cheesecake at Bens?" I'd been so excited to share a proper New York cheesecake at my favorite Montreal diner when Franck first arrived, but it was a letdown, to put it mildly. He thought it was the most disgusting thing he'd ever tasted. You win some, you lose some.

Franck chuckled. "Cheesecake is unimaginably awful."

"For a French person."

He rolled his eyes upwards towards the somewhat grubby ceiling of the deli. "Anyway, back to my point. I worry there may be a chasm of experience between me and everyone in France. Will we still be able to relate to one another like before?"

He had a point. I wasn't sure either how this new Canadian Franck would fly with all the folks back in Villers-la-Faye.

"You want to know the scariest thing of all?"

"Of course."

His eyebrows drew together. "The last time we were at Bens and you convinced me to try a forkful of your cheesecake, I actually didn't find it so bad after all—"

I slapped the Formica tabletop and laughed. "What!? Shhhhh...lower your voice. The walls have ears, and the consulate will for sure confiscate your French passport if they hear that."

Franck grinned. "It just goes to show, I really *have* changed."

"And if your family don't like it, guess who will be blamed for it?" I pointed my fork at myself before Franck could answer.

"Nobody will blame you Laura," he said.

I sighed. "Maybe, but you wouldn't be here if it wasn't for me. I'm a logical scapegoat for the fact they haven't seen you in so long, that they miss you desperately, and that you've changed."

Before I knew Franck and his family better, I would have just assumed that Franck's family—like mine—admired and encouraged such things as travel and living independently abroad. In my world, this was seen as a crucial step to growing up and starting an adult life.

I was shocked when I learned Franck's family—and indeed, most people I knew in France—did not share that world view. In Burgundy, especially in Franck's case, the prevailing goal was to keep one's family and especially one's children as close by as humanly possible, preferably within a one-kilometer radius from the family home or, better yet, right next door.

When Franck left his village the previous November to come and join me in Québec, his family were convinced they would never see him again. Mémé had a cousin at the turn of the century who left for the United States and subsequently vanished. That tale was trotted out with alarming frequency at family meals and I often found myself wondering if it was for my benefit.

"But that was before commercial air travel!" I would protest. "And a functioning postal system!"

No-one listened. They all felt Franck would be sucked irretrievably into the vortex of the wild new world, thanks to me.

Our pastrami sandwiches arrived, and they smelled rich and meaty, like they always did. I squirted roughly half a bottle of yellow mustard on the side of my plate to use as a dip and dug in. The pillowy slices of soft rye bread were the perfect foil for the thin slices of perfectly seasoned smoked beef inside. Neither of us said anything else for a while, but contentment reigned.

When we were left with only our pickles, I chewed on mine thoughtfully. It was briny, fermenting perfection. "Do you think your family are actually going to let you leave when it's time to come back to Montréal?"

"I already left once before, and I'll do it again. I'm my own man Laura. They'll have no choice."

I dipped the chewed end of my pickle in my leftover mustard and took a crispy bite. As far as I was concerned, Franck underestimated both the ties of his home and the ability of his family to pull a major guilt trip on him. "We'll see."

"Is focusing on presents your way of coping?" Franck asked, his left eyebrow raised.

He'd only figured that out now? "Of course it is."

"In that case, I promise you I will not utter a word of complaint about the inevitable weight of the suitcases I know I'll be obliged to carry."

There was no point in denying that would indeed be the case. "*Merci.*"

"Consider it a proof of love." He took his paper napkin and

wiped off a streak of yellow mustard that had somehow got on my thumb.

"I will," I said. "I do."

"Will you show me the presents when we get back home...to our gloriously empty home?"

"Yes, and I'm sure we can find other things besides that to keep us busy tonight, seeing as we'll have the whole place to ourselves."

Franck winked at me. "I like where this is headed." He raised his hand to get the waiter's attention. "Check please!"

chapter three

The disembodied voice boomed over the speaker in one of McGill's many gymnasiums. "Put your pens and pencils down!"

I wrote one last word, 'Troilus' in my final exam essay on Shakespeare's rather obscure play Troilus and Cressida. Only then did I place my pen down on my exam paper.

I was massaging my palm as I took a really good look at my pen. It had been brand-new at the beginning of the exam—I had a superstitious thing about treating myself to new stationary for exams, feeling somehow as though it conferred some special brand of luck—but now it was chewed up and chunks were broken off. Gnawing on a pen helped me think, and this one was only suited to the garbage can now. Even with my new-pen luck, this round of exams had felt mixed at best.

Of the exams I'd written, I thought this last one, for my Survey of Shakespeare, was probably my best work, but then again Professor Shaw was a brutal marker. It was anybody's guess how I would do.

I had written non-stop for three hours and even with my palm massage, my right hand felt as though it was frozen into a claw. Anyway, I wouldn't know the grades until I came back from Christmas vacation. This meant my next stop was France.

I tapped my heels against the varnished wooden floor and waited for one of the assistant examiners to come and pick my exam up from my table. My heart sunk as I saw she'd started her collection on the opposite side of the gym.

I'd packed my things and was already daydreaming about

my first café in Beaune, my first glass of kir, my first slice of *saucisson sec…*

Franck and I had our departure organized down to the minute. I just had enough time to finish my exam and rush to the bus depot in order to catch our bus to Mirabel airport—way out in the fields almost an hour away from downtown Montréal. *If only the examiner would hurry up and collect my paper.*

Franck was bringing our suitcases, and I must have reminded him fifty times not to forget the blue duffel bag that I'd put in the middle of our bed.

It contained all of my presents, aka peace offerings, for Franck's family. They were beautifully wrapped and carefully packed. I'd underlined the importance of the blue duffel bag to Franck that morning with many dramatic hand gestures and colorful threats.

Thank God, she picked up my exam. I was good to go. Outside the gymnasium where many of the Arts exams were held, the cold bit my face and the ground was one huge ice rink.

In Villers-la-Faye, the vineyards would be bare, but there would still be grass growing between many of the rows. I craved the color green in all its variations. Montréal was just so white and gray once the snow started—beautiful in its own way but not what I was used to.

I pushed open the huge swinging door to the McGill metro station and took the escalator to the platforms below ground. My heart beat fast in my throat. Finally, we were going back to where it all began for Franck and me. It felt momentous…and scary.

When, twenty minutes later, I remerged from the metro to the bus station platform and saw Franck's eyes glowing above his scarf in anticipation, I knew this was far more important for him than it was for me. It had been too long. It had to go well. It was up to me to make sure of that.

We were only fifteen minutes away from Mirabel airport and we had chattered for most of the ride, covering the topics of how nice it was at the apartment without Ava, how slippery the sidewalks were, and how my Shakespeare exam had gone. We made out for a bit after reminiscing about the first time Franck had been on this bus when I'd picked him up at the airport. We hadn't seen each other in months.

"You remembered all our luggage?" I asked, after a time.

"*Oui* Laura," he said with mock patience. "It's all safely in the belly of the bus. See? You didn't need to nag me so much."

"Didn't I?" I asked, with an arched brow. I'd been living with Franck for a year now and he still refused to accept that he was disorganized and constantly losing things—his wallet, his keys, his gloves...he'd even lost his permanent residency papers in a bar when he first arrived in Montréal.

Franck's right leg was bouncing up and down with nervous energy. "Oh!" he said suddenly. "Oh no!"

My heart skipped a beat. "What?"

"I forgot my passport on your desk."

"What!?" I shrieked, causing several other heads to turn in our direction. "Are you serious? How could you?" I checked my watch, my mind going a million miles an hour already. "We'll never have time to get back and pick it up and then get to Mirabel again in time for our flight. We'll have to rebook and—"

He put his hand on my leg. "I was just teasing you. It's right here." He extracted it from the top pocket of his parka.

I punched his thigh. "That's not funny," I muttered.

"Wasn't it?" Franck asked, and arched his brow just like I had. "I beg to differ."

"No, it was *not*. I'm now obliged to run through a checklist, and it's entirely your fault."

"No," he groaned. "Not the checklist."

"Yes, the checklist. Don't whinge. Here we go. I have my passport. You do in fact have yours. Correct?"

"Correct." He rolled his eyes.

"Plane tickets?"

Franck's eyes went huge and he began frantically patting his pockets.

"No!" I growled, half disbelieving, half furious. "Are you serious? How can you have forgotten our plane tickets? We'll never—"

He started chuckling again. "I was just joking."

I crossed my arms over my chest and sat heavily back in my seat, not even deigning to give him a response.

"I'm sorry," he said, after his mirth had subsided a bit. "You're just so fun to rile up. I can't resist."

I cast him a baleful stare.

"Don't be mad," he said, cajoling. He picked up my left hand and tried to unpry my fingers from the tight fist they formed. When this failed, he lifted my arm up and began to press the lightest butterfly kisses inside my wrist and along my inner arm. They sent shivers—the good kind—everywhere, but there was no way I was going to let him know. I was determined to be an ice queen. Packing was no laughing matter.

"Laura, *mon amour*," he murmured. "I apologize for teasing you. I just can't resist how your eyes flash."

"Hmph." *Ice queen.*

"Besides, you *did* nag me a lot."

"I had no choice! Whether you admit it or not, the fact is you're absent-minded. I want this trip to go well. I'm not even going to ask you if you remembered the duffel bag of presents, because that is one thing I *did* nag you enough about. There's no way you would have forgotten those."

Franck dropped my hand. His breath caught.

I shook my head. "Nope. I'm not falling for it a third time."

"I can't believe I forgot the presents," he said on a gasp.

He was really playing this little game for all it was worth, wasn't he? "Nice try."

"No...Laura...I'm serious. I don't know how, but I really did forget them."

I snorted. "Yeah, right. I bet they're still on our bed, *n'est-ce pas?*"

He nodded, his eyes haunted. He was doing a good job of acting convincing. Thank God I could make out the blocky white buildings and air traffic tower of the airport in the distance. "Do the French learn that fable about the Boy Who Called Wolf?"

"*Non*...," he said. "But this time I'm not lying—"

"Stop it. I'll tell you the fable some time, but for now I can tell you that you are that boy calling wolf, and it's not pretty. There's no way you could have forgotten the presents. I've spent weeks picking them out and wrapping them. I just found the perfect thing for your Dad yesterday—a beautiful photo book about the workshops of famous painters like Monet, Matisse, Gaugin...all the Impressionists your parents like. The bag was huge and sitting in the middle of our bed. Even if you were blind—"

"I'm serious Laura. I took all the other suitcases out on the sidewalk and was just about to go back into the apartment and grab the duffel bag, but the taxi arrived. I locked up and completely forgot to go back and get it."

I frowned at Franck. That mischievous glint in his eye had vanished, along with the tell-tale quirk of his lips.

"That's just not possible," I said. "I must have reminded you twenty times."

"I'm so sorry." Franck squeezed my arm just as the bus squealed to a stop in front of the *Départs* terminal.

I still didn't know what to believe. I could easily picture him taking the duffel bag out from the belly of the bus along with our other suitcases and laughing that he'd hoodwinked me. I gathered my stuff. "We only have fifteen minutes to get to our gate," I said. "We have to hurry."

Franck bounded down the bus alley ahead of me. I joined him in the crowd of people waiting for their luggage to be unloaded from the bus. My suitcase came off. Franck's suitcase came off.

Franck turned to me with an apologetic expression. "*On y a*," he said, gesturing to the door to the terminal with his thumb.

"But...the presents."

"I told you, I forgot them. I'm so, so sorry."

Oh my God. He was serious. How could he do this? How

could I arrive empty-handed? It was unthinkable. "You weren't joking?"

He shook his head slowly. "Not about that. I'm so sorry. I know how much time and energy and work you put into those presents, and I so appreciate it. If I could go back in time and remember the duffel bag, I would."

Anger rose up inside me like an erupting volcano. I didn't get mad often, but when I did, I was ripe for murder.

I turned on my heel and stalked into the terminal, deaf to Franck's pleading and numerous apologies. It should have been a special moment, boarding a plane together for the first time, but I knew if I opened my mouth pure vitriol would come spewing out. I never knew ice princesses could have so much boiling lava roiling inside.

I didn't speak to Franck again until we were somewhere over Iceland.

I spent hours as we flew up over Atlantic Canada, then the Atlantic and then Greenland, inwardly raging, then I tried to sleep but failed. It was exhausting being so angry, and it was even more exhausting to have the person I was angry at sitting right beside me in a narrow airplane seat.

That was the weird thing about love. When we first met, I couldn't remember ever being furious with Franck in those first few months, but now… he sometimes did things that drove me crazy and vice versa. I still hadn't reconciled how I could love someone so much—if anything our love had grown and deepened in Montréal—yet find them so infuriating at times. Sometimes, like right then, the emotions felt too big for my body.

As the tide of my anger began to ebb, I began to see things with a little more perspective. Franck was so absent-minded that I believed his mistake was sincere, even though it was idiotic.

I could tell by the dark expression on his features that he felt terribly. Still, I couldn't stop ruminating over those beautiful, hand-picked presents sitting useless and sad in our freezing bedroom.

Now his family would think I hadn't even thought of them, that as well as stealing their Franck I was an ungrateful guest. I wanted to unwind the spool of time and whisper in Franck's ear to go back into our apartment and get the duffel bag before jumping in the taxi. It wasn't the material things in themselves I was upset about forgetting, it was all the thought I'd put into them. I'd been so excited to for everyone to open their presents on Christmas morning. Good god, arriving empty handed for Christmas? My mother would be horrified, and my maternal grandmother would disown me.

When I opened my eyes after a fruitless attempt at sleep, Franck was watching me. "Did you sleep?"

"A bit," I lied, my voice rough.

His shoulders dropped. "Are you talking to me again?"

"I guess," I said. "But I'm still upset."

"Of course you are." He stroked my hair. "Anything else would be very out-of-character."

I didn't know quite how to take that. "I feel like I could still kill you," I warned him.

He clicked his tongue. "That's fair. It's okay."

"Now you see why I have to nag you so much."

He cocked his head. "Actually...I'm not so sure about that. From a Cartesian perspective, I wonder if the fact I forgot the duffel bag proved it had a contrary effect—" He stopped talking when he saw the look I cast his way.

"Right." He nodded, still caressing my hand. "I will shut up until further notice."

"I might start stapling reminder notes to your forehead." That thought gave me the first smile I'd had since Franck told me about the duffel bag.

"You know what? I wouldn't even complain." He leaned over and gave me a gentle kiss that melted my ire a little bit more. "Truce?"

"Truce," I grumbled. "But you need to take the blame with your family that we have nothing for them."

He nodded now, an image of pious repentance comparable to that of the Pope. "Of course. I promise to give a full confession of my sins. *C'est normal.*"

"Who's picking us up in Paris?" I asked. I'd been so preoccupied with my exams that I'd completely forgotten to ask.

"My parents, I guess," Franck said. "They told me someone would be coming, but they hadn't quite figured out who yet."

It was a three-hour drive in each direction between Villers-la-Faye and Charles de Gaulle airport in Paris, and I knew the Franck's retiring father André was terrified of driving in the lawless maw of Parisian traffic. "We could have just taken a taxi from the airport to the Gare de Lyon and then the TGV down to Dijon or Beaune."

Franck shook his head. "I've been away too long for that. I'm coming home, which many of my family—most of them actually—probably thought I would never do. This is a big deal."

"I guess I didn't think that through." Lurking at the back of my mind was the unwelcome thought that if his arrival was such a momentous event, his departure would be no less so...if they let him leave with me at all.

As I was mulling this over, the cabin steward brought us our breakfasts. My heart leapt when I opened up the lid of mine. There sat three miniature pastries—a pain au chocolat, a croissant, and a *pain aux raisins*, and my own little mini baguette on a white china plate. Next to it was two tiny jars of Bonne Maman jam—raspberry and Reine Claude. With that there were two little squares of unsalted butter from Brittany.

I sighed as I took in the welcome sight. "I think I love Air France." I felt as though I had already arrived. My favorite breakfast had always been a French breakfast of pastries, jam, and black coffee. Savory things at breakfast like eggs and bacon made me want to gag.

There was even a little triangle of camembert from Normandie and a large chunk of Emmenthal hiding underneath my napkin. Oh happy day.

"Ah," Franck echoed my sigh as he stared down at his platter. "La France. *My* France. You are so beautiful."

"Are you talking to your food?"

"Of course."

"You don't usually do that."

Franck grinned at me. "Maybe it's because I haven't recently come across any food that's worth talking to."

chapter four

We disembarked at Charles de Gaulle at roughly six o'clock in the morning, Paris time. My previous memories of the airport came flooding back.

There were those incessant three chimes playing over the intercom system with barely intelligible announcements following. Here were the weird futurist tubes that conveyed us from the arrivals level to the baggage claim. There was also that thickness in the air that came from hundreds of passengers lighting up their cigarettes on arrival, even though there were "*Défense de Fumer*" signs all over the place, and only half of them were defaced with graffiti.

A wave of fatigue hit me as we stood by the luggage carrousel waiting for it to begin to turn and spit off our suitcases. We'd been waiting a ridiculously long time already. I rocked backwards on my feet.

Franck grabbed my arm to steady me. "Hey, are you all right?"

I blinked and shook my head. "Just really tired. I could curl up on the floor right here and fall asleep in under ten seconds."

Franck peered down at the floor, which was grubby with two crushed cigarette butts and a suspicious brown streak smeared over the tiles in front of where we stood. "Trust me, you don't want to lie down on this floor."

The French people around us were cursing and complaining about the sheer ineptitude of the management of Charles de Gaulle airport. Some particularly animated ones shook their fists at the intercom speakers. Living with Franck I had become inured to the French love for complaining about things, or "*râler*" as the French call it, with affection. It was a national pastime in France (after drinking and eating, *bien sûr*).

"Didn't you sleep on the flight?" Franck asked.

"No. Did you?"

"For a few hours I think."

A fat lot of good the not-speaking to Franck thing had done me. "How could you sleep when you knew I was so mad at you?"

Franck shrugged. "I knew you would forgive me at some point. I just had to wait it out. It's a shame you couldn't sleep though."

"I was far too *angry* to sleep," I ground out.

"I'm sorry for that. I'll take special care of you now." He anchored me against him with his arm tightly around me while he smoked with his other hand. I was simply too tired to be angry any longer.

From what I could tell from the way Franck raced off the plane and into the terminal, not smoking for seven hours for a smoker wasn't an easy feat. I hoped one day he would quit, but it surely wouldn't be over the next few weeks when we would be surrounded by all his family and friends—the majority of whom smoked just as much or more than Franck.

"It's amazing," I said after a while. "I actually understand everything people are saying in French this time, even the people with accents. It's so different from the first time I arrived here at the beginning of my exchange year when I couldn't understand a thing. I was so lost. I couldn't even remember the French word for "yellow". It's a surreal thing to learn a language later in life, *n'est-ce pas*?"

"You did a better job than me," Franck said. "You speak French very well, but even though I understand English now I don't think I'll ever get rid of my accent."

I wanted to reassure Franck that he would, but honestly, I wasn't convinced. Aside from the born and bred *Montréalais*, who truly were completely bilingual, most French people I knew had a difficult time making English sounds. That never seemed to go away.

"Maybe not." I grabbed his chin and gave him a kiss. "But it's extremely charming."

Then, a miracle happened. The luggage carrousel began to turn with a fingernails-on-the-chalkboard screech and our bags eventually rolled off.

"I think I need an espresso," I said. "Or several."

"I'm sure we can do that once we get through customs and immigration."

Uh. I'd forgotten about that. Although I was dead on my feet, Franck was thrumming with excitement and I couldn't blame him. How incredible it was for him to reunite with his family—I knew how much he'd missed them. A huge bubble of joy rose in me and, in that moment, the presents didn't feel nearly as important as they had in Montréal.

Franck walked fast out of the luggage area and made a bee-way for the immigration and customs line-up. I was practically running to keep up with his long, quick strides, but I didn't feel I could ask him to slow down—not with his family waiting on the other side.

All his hurrying meant we were only twenty people or so from the front of the line. When I looked up, I saw that we were waiting in the line-up for "All Passports". The line-up right beside us, for "French passports" wasn't in fact a line-up at all. People were quickly walking through and flashing their passports to a bored looking immigration officer who just kept waving them along, probably so he could go on his break.

"You should hop over there," I said, indicating the French line-up to Franck with a nod. "Your family is dying to see you, and this might take a while. I'll catch up."

The officer in our line seemed to be talking to every single person who went up to his booth. We crawled forward at a snail's pace compared to the Indy 500 race occurring beside us.

Franck looked over and then shook his head. "No," he said. "I'll wait. We'll go through together."

The last thing I wanted was to feel like I was holding Franck back one second longer than necessary, or for his family to think that. “Really,” I said. “I’m fine. Go ahead.”

I could tell every atom within him was wanting to break into a run towards the door, but he shook his head again, resolute. I’d seen that stubborn look on his face before. “Absolutely not. I left France to find you again. There’s no way I’m returning without you on my arm.”

I flung my arms around him. “*Je t’aime*,” I said. “Even if you did forget the presents.”

He kissed the top of my head. “*Je t’aime aussi.*”

We finally got to the front of the line and chatted briefly and politely with the officer. Franck was chomping at the bit but in line I’d warned him of something I’d learned working as a Customs Officer during the summer—if a passenger was going to waste my time or be rude, I would waste theirs. Tit for tat. I was fairly certain this was a worldwide phenomenon.

We got through. Franck still held tightly on to my hand, and he dragged me along in his wake. He was almost running now.

Who was going to be there waiting for us? Just André? Perhaps André and Michèle and Franck’s little brother Emmanuel-Marie? Whatever it was going to be, it would start happening in five seconds, four, three, two, one…we burst through the sliding doors.

There, pressed against the gate and holding the rest of the crowd at bay, were roughly thirty of Franck’s family members, laughing, weeping, dancing, and breaking out into a spontaneous *ban bourgignon.*

I lost track of Franck within seconds. We were both swept up into a flurry of *bisous* and hugs and exclamations. There was no choice but to go along with it. I hugged and kissed back, barely aware of who I was greeting, it was all such a blur of emotion and noise. There was Mémé, and Tante Renée, and Jacqueline, and Jean, and even Stéphanie—Franck's sister who had set us up on a blind date in the first place.

Part of me was in shock that I was back here with them again. In France. Many times since I travelled back to Canada after my exchange year was over it had all felt like a dream. I hated that feeling—it never failed to panic my soul when I doubted that my wonderful, life-changing year hadn't existed in the first place.

But it had. Franck was the proof. And his family surrounding me, grabbing at my arms and jacket and kissing me on every inch of my face, was the proof. I'd never seen such a hero's welcome. It was staggering.

Mémé had finally stopped dancing and was now clinging to Franck, her arms locked around his neck. "*Quelle joie*!" She said, her eyes misty. "My Franckie has come back to me."

Jacqueline and Renée began to herd our mob in the direction of the parking garage attached to the airport. "How will we all fit in the cars?" I asked the nearest person, Franck's uncle Bernard who I'd only met once before.

Renée, dressed in a sweeping chartreuse shawl, majestic as always, threw her hands up and laughed a booming laugh that turned the heads of strangers. "We are travelling in a veritable welcome convoy!" she cried. "Five cars. Like gypsies! How glorious is that!?"

"Wow," I murmured. As I was dragged along by Renée's arm linked jauntily in mine, I realized my wooziness had gotten worse. The white marble floor of the airport tilted up at bizarre angles and I kept having to blink to keep my eyes open. When was the last time I slept? That morning...or was it the previous morning, in Montréal? I'd written an exam, fought with Franck, flew 3,400 miles across the Atlantic, and was now being swept along in Paris with a loving bunch of garrulous French people. It had been, all in all, quite a day.

Whichever car they put me in I knew I would fall almost instantly into a dead sleep. I went on my tiptoes once we'd reached the parking garage to try and catch sight of Franck, but he was nowhere to be seen. He had to be somewhere amongst all those people.

I was manhandled into the back seat of Jean and Jacqueline's Renault Espace. I knew in my heart they were acting with enthusiasm and love, but part of me couldn't help feel like a kidnap victim shoved in the rear of an unmarked van.

I waited for Franck slide in beside me, but instead Mémé and Renée climbed in and bracketed me in the back seat. Jean took the steering wheel and Jacqueline joined him up front in the passenger seat as his co-pilot.

"Where's Franck?" I asked, as Jean turned the key in the ignition.

"Oh!" Renée waved her hand in one of her flamboyant gestures. "He's driving down with his parents and Emmanuel-Marie. We only have two returning *Canadiens*, so we decided to share you between the cars!"

As much as I adored Franck's family, I couldn't help but feel a bit abandoned. This was worsened by the fact that I wanted nothing more than to sleep. If Franck was here, he could keep up the conversation—he'd slept on the flight. Damn. I'd never gotten that espresso that I so desperately needed to keep me awake.

"Are you tired?" Jacqueline turned around and asked me over her shoulder.

I considered lying and giving the polite answer, but I knew I wouldn't be able to hide it. Plus, I must have looked like something out of the twilight zone with my scraggly hair and red eyes. "Exhausted," I said. "So sleepy."

"Don't worry!" Mémé laughed and squeezed my arm. "We have so many questions! We will keep you awake."

I didn't think anything short of a fire alarm could keep me awake once Jean got out of this parking garage and started driving on the autoroute down to Burgundy. Still, the polite Canadian was well-engrained in me, and the idea of snoring through their questions dismayed me to my core. "Could we stop somewhere where I can drink a quick espresso?" I asked. "Or five?"

Jacqueline laughed gaily. "I know a perfect autoroute station just a few kilometers from here. We could all do with a *pétit café.*"

"But the others might not know where we've gone to!" Mémé protested.

"They'll be following us," Jacqueline said. "I'm sure they'll turn off too."

"Not the way André drives," grumbled Mémé. "He drives like an octogenarian and I can say that because I am one. I'm sure we'll lose him almost immediately."

There was daylight ahead, and suddenly we were on the road away from Charles de Gaulle. It was slow moving with traffic, of course, and Jean was leaning on the horn, because this was Paris, and honking was a matter of form.

"So!" Mémé slung her thin, muscular arm around my shoulders. "Tell us everything."

Jean and Jacqueline spent the next twenty minutes debating the attributes of different autoroute stations. I felt like screaming that I really didn't care, as long as they served strong espressos.

In the back, Renée and Mémé peppered me with question after question. "What is Franck's favorite thing to eat in Montréal?"

"Ummm...well, he certainly missed French food."

Renée snorted. "Of course he did! How could he not? French food is the best food in the world."

"But he does like the Montréal smoked meat sandwiches."

This intrigued Renée. She was always fascinated by food and cooking, so I had to explain smoked meat in great detail, as well as the ambiance at Schwartz's. I did all of this while feeling as though I was floating somewhere outside my body. My mouth was sounding out the words like a puppet's, and it was becoming harder and harder for me to move the strings properly. If I could close my eyes, just for second...

"Do you have a good *boulangerie* near you?" Mémé asked.

How was I to explain to a French person that everyone in the world didn't eat baguettes at every meal? I was far too tired for such an onerous task. "We don't eat baguettes very often," I said. "But we do eat bagels."

"Bagels?" Renée exclaimed. "What are bagels? You must tell me everything about this."

"They're round," I yawned. My eyelids were falling...falling...

Abruptly, Jean cranked the wheel and veered into the exit lane of the highway.

Jacqueline shrieked. "Jean!"

"I forgot about this one," Jean said, unflappable as usual. "I remembered at the last minute. They serve excellent *pain aux raisins*."

Ahhh. Caffeine wasn't far away now. My stomach grumbled to get some attention. Now that I thought about it, that breakfast on the plane felt like a long time ago.

Jacqueline peered out her window. "Did André and the others manage to follow us? You turned so suddenly Jean, it's not like you gave them much notice. I swear—."

"I see their car," Jean said. "It's fine."

We found a parking slot just in front of the *station d'autoroute,* which in France traditionally included a coffee bar as well as a restaurant and gift shop. As I climbed out of the car, I wasn't moving half as spryly as Mémé was.

André's car pulled up beside Jean's van. Franck leapt out before André had come to a complete stop. He made a beeline to me and gave me a kiss. "How are you doing? I didn't know they'd been planning to drive us down in different cars. They shoved me in there before I knew what was going on."

"Same," I said. "But it's fine." Even though I wasn't feeling it, I had to be magnanimous about this. It was a good thing for Franck to catch up with his family without me around for a bit. "It's just that I'm exhausted and they have soooooo many questions. I'm literally falling asleep as I try to answer them. I need some espressos."

"More than one?" Franck hitched a brow.

"Definitely. I'm also starving."

"Me too."

We went inside surrounded by a crowd of family who had all decided it was time to take some refreshment as well. There were cousins I'd only met once or twice and some people I didn't recognize at all.

Franck parked me at a round, bar height table by the coffee bar. "What do you want to eat?"

"Pain au chocolate if they have one," I said. "Or any other pastry."

"Done," he said. "You stay here."

Stéphanie, Franck's sister, materialized beside me. "Stéph!" I cried with relief. "I barely had time to say hello to you at the airport. Are you in the car with Franck?"

She shook her head. "No, I'm driving back down with les Buffenoir." Ah, that was Franck's hilarious quarter uncle (it was a long story) who had a son and a daughter close to our age. I'd also caught a glimpse of them as we were herded through the airport.

I leaned closer to her. "Steph," I confessed. "I'm so tired."

Her brows drew together over her expressive hazel eyes. "Oh no," she said. "Poor you. None of us have travelled that far before, so I guess we don't really understand what it feels like."

"I haven't truly slept in." I counted my fingers. "Almost twenty-four hours."

"Ugh," she groaned. "What are you going to do about the champagne tasting?"

That jolted me awake. "Champagne tasting? What are you talking about?"

"Didn't they tell you? Jacqueline has planned for all of us to stop off at their favorite Champagne maker for a big tasting. Jean and Jacqueline and a few of the others needed to pick up champagne before the holidays and it's on our route down...well, not *exactly* I guess, but good champagne is worth the detour."

I was still trying to figure out how to respond to this news when Franck arrived with four espressos for me, lined up in little glass cups with metal handles. He slid me a bakery bag with a steaming pain au chocolate and a *pain au raisin* inside."

"Four espressos enough, *ma puce*?" He looked at me over the rim of his espresso cup with a gleam in his eyes.

He thought I couldn't handle four espressos? Had he ever even *met* me? "I'll let you know."

"I got you a *pain au raisin* too," he said. "Jean tells me they are excellent here."

"Yes, the stop was rather...ah...unexpected."

"Jean's a terrible driver." Stéphanie shook her head. "There's a reason I'm not riding in his van."

Wonderful. I downed one of the espressos to fortify myself. It only took two gulps, really.

"Have you heard anything about a champagne tasting?" I asked Franck.

"No," Franck said. "What are you talking about?"

Jacqueline sidled up just then. "It was going to be a surprise, but it looks as though the cat's out of the bag." She frowned at Stéphanie. "I've arranged for a tasting at Clos de la Chapelle on the way down...you remember our *fétiche* champagne makers."

"Uh...that's lovely." Franck's eyes rolled over to me. "But it's in Ville-Dommange, isn't? That's quite a way off the route down to Burgundy."

"It's not every day we go to the airport to pick up world travelers!" Jacqueline buffeted both our backs with a hearty slap. "It's an occasion, so we made a fun day out of it!"

I downed my second espresso.

"*Bien sûr*," Franck agreed. "How marvelous. It's always a good time for champagne."

Jacqueline kissed his cheek soundly. "Now, there's my nephew who I know and love! For a second there you had me scared with your lack of enthusiasm about champagne. Why, you've always *loved* champagne."

My third espresso went down the hatch. It was dawning on me that the champagne tasting was happening, and that I was going to have to stay awake for far longer than I'd anticipated.

"I do love champagne," Franck admitted.

"Of course you do! It was imperative we welcome you back to France in the proper fashion," Jacqueline said. "Otherwise we'll never lure you back here!" She bubbled up with laughter and went over to talk to Franck's cousin's husband.

Lure Franck back to France? If that was their plan, Jacqueline and the others were not exactly going about it in a particularly clandestine fashion.

The caffeine had started to hit my nervous system. Maybe I could stay awake. Besides, Franck was right. There was no bad time for champagne. Stéphanie drifted off to help her mother locate Emmanuel-Marie.

I drank my final espresso. Franck winced at me. "Sorry."

"It's fine. How could I possibly complain about a champagne tasting in Champagne?" The last thing I wanted to be was a killjoy. I just needed a mental kick, and maybe a pastry.

I took a bite of warm pain au chocolat. The flakes of the butter-rich pastry melted on my tongue, combining with the melty chocolate filling. I groaned. Nobody did pain au chocolat like the French. It was extraordinary that one could find such sublime pastries in what was basically the French version of a truck stop.

Franck took a deep suck of his Gitane. "Don't start groaning like that. I may be tired, but I'm not dead."

Fixing my eyes on his, I took another glorious bite and savored it slowly. I groaned again, but a bit more softly so only he could hear.

He drew in a shaky breath. "Maybe it's a good thing we're traveling in separate cars. Do you need more espressos?"

I surveyed my four empty cups. In Montréal I was used to drinking huge thermoses of coffee in class, so I still felt like I needed a bit more, even though the muddy espresso was far stronger than the watered down coffee I bought every morning from the coffee stand on campus. "Please," I said. "Two more...no, wait...maybe three?"

Stéphanie had joined us again and frowned at me. "Seven

espressos? Laura, are you crazy? Your heart is going to give out!"

I shook my head. "Nah. I'll be fine."

"Are you sure?" Franck asked.

"You're familiar with the amount of coffee I consume in Montréal, right?"

"But these are much, much stronger Laura," he reminded me.

I waved a hand. "I'll be fine. Trust me." I finished off my pain au chocolat, then turned to my *pain aux raisins*. It was pillowy soft with the slightest crunch of caramelized sugar between the coils of the fresh flaky pastry with sweet tender raisins to complete the whole. What did you know? Jean was right. These were the best *pain aux raisins* I'd ever tasted.

chapter five

A little over an hour later we pulled up in front of the Clos de la Chappelle winery in the beautiful village of Ville-Dommange.

On the way in, I saw the entire village was decorated with fresh cut greenery with lights strung everywhere. The Domaine itself was a thing of beauty—constructed of piled golden stone and surrounded on three sides by rolling vineyards. The vines were bare right now, of course, as they had gone into hibernation for the winter, but without leaves they possessed a certain undeniable stark beauty.

The window boxes that undoubtably showed off bright red geraniums in the summer months were now filled with artfully arranged greenery and branches, intertwined with what looked like fairy lights.

I was wide awake and more than ready for the champagne tasting. In fact, the seven espressos had left me with the unusual sensation of vibrating, but I could hide that from the others.

An attractive woman emerged from the building through a massive wooden door that looked as though it dated roughly from the fifteenth century. We were in France now, I reminded myself, so it probably did. She was dressed in a slim cut, ankle-length woolen skirt and a cheery red sweater that looked like cashmere. I was glad there were no mirrors around, as I didn't even want to think about what I looked like given that I had neither showered nor slept since Montréal. Ignorance was bliss in that regard.

Besides, as the various family members arrived *en masse* and tumbled out of their cars, I realized I could easily stay anonymous in such a hoard.

The woman held out her hands to Jean and Jacqueline and kissed them both warmly on their cheeks—not twice like we did in Burgundy, but four times.

Franck appeared beside me with Mémé on his arm.

She pulled him closer and laughed to me, "I'm never going to let him go!" I tried to convince myself she just meant it in jest. Franck had always been her favorite grandchild, after all. Everyone knew it, although Mémé insisted on denying she had a favorite.

"Did you sleep?" Franck asked.

"Of course she didn't!" Mémé swatted his arm. "There was no time for that! We had so many questions, and we're not done yet."

Franck's eyes widened at me.

"*C'est vrai*," I said. "There's *no end* to the questions, but luckily those espressos seem to have done the trick."

"Are you jittery?" His free hand brushed against mine.

I curled my fingers in a fist so he couldn't see my hands shake. "Not at all," I said, breezily.

Franck tilted his head and lifted my hand up. He unbent my fingers with his thumb. My hand shook in his, even though I concentrated with every atom of my being to stop it.

"Not jittery, *hein*?"

I clamped my mouth together. I did feel a bit like I was going to jump out of my own skin, but surely that would pass.

"Jittery?" Mémé leaned over and took my hand from Franck. Her skin was thin and crepey, but I felt the strength that was there, and I knew there was no point at all in trying to slip my hand out of hers. "Why is Laura jittery?"

"She drank seven espressos at the autoroute stop." Franck answered. "I was impressed. That has to be some sort of record."

"Seven espressos!" Mémé slapped me gently on the arm. "You're going to stroke out."

"No, no," I reassured her. "I'm used to drinking a lot of

coffee. And at least I'm not falling asleep anymore. In fact, I have quite a lot of energy—my second wind, I guess."

"More like a caffeine hurricane," Franck muttered.

"Shhhh." Mémé swatted at us to be quiet. "I need to hear this."

Jacqueline and the champagne lady were discussing the pros and cons of doing a tour of the Domaine and the cellars or cutting right to the chase with the tasting.

"Let me ask my Canadians!" Jacqueline beckoned Franck and I over.

We greeted the woman with polite handshakes, and I did my best to keep my distance. I was sure I smelled as grungy as I felt. So much for staying anonymous.

"This is Laura and Franck," Jacqueline said. "Our Canadians. Laura is a Canadian—actually born there, can you imagine?—and our Franck went to go to live with her Montréal so they could be reunited."

The champagne woman clutched her hands to her cashmere sweater. "How romantic! That is just wonderful. Canada! How exciting! I want to hear all about it, but first, would you prefer to go straight to the tasting or do the tour of the cellars and the Domaine?"

She waited expectantly, but I knew my answer. "Going straight to the tasting might be the best," I said. "We've been travelling for almost twenty-four hours and at a certain point we're not going to be able to stay awake any longer."

Jacqueline jerked back and Franck trod meaningfully on my foot. What? I had answered honestly, and it was *true* that we were both going to hit a wall, even if I seemed to be the only one who had travelled enough to know the inevitability of that.

"Who wants to go to the tasting directly?" Jacqueline turned and asked the assembled family, who were all chatting amongst themselves.

"*Nous! Nous! Moi*!" They all shouted in a rag-tag chorus. Thank God, I wasn't in the minority.

Franck gave me a pointed look, his forehead creased. Surely I couldn't be the only one who wanted to sit down and drink some champagne sooner rather than later?"

The champagne lady clapped her hands together. "Let's taste then!" she said. "Follow me."

Jacqueline frowned at me before following the lady.

"What?" I hissed to Franck. "What did I do wrong?"

"You should have picked the tour. That's what they wanted you to do."

"They why did they ask?" I was so confused.

"For form's sake."

"What? But why did they want us to pick the tour? Surely that would just be more work for the lady?"

"It's polite to take interest in things like that, especially because Jacqueline set it up."

I clutched my forehead. "Why didn't you tell me that? How was I supposed to know?"

Franck shrugged. "It's just...isn't it obvious? It's the only polite choice to make."

"It's not obvious to *me*." Us Canadians were polite about many things that the French were not i.e. not cutting in front of someone in a line, avoiding verbal conflict in conversation, not double or triple parking and blocking in other cars...how was I supposed to know that opting out of a tour was considered impolite?

"Look, I don't know about you, but I'm exhausted and wired. I'm not thinking straight. When the caffeine in my system dissipates, I am going to crash *hard*. I've done it before, and it is not pretty. Nothing short of a meteor hitting the earth beside me is going to keep me awake. Isn't it better to go straight to the tasting than actually fall asleep in the middle of the tour?"

Franck frowned as he mulled this over.

"I'm doing my best," I said. "I'm just so damn tired, and I honestly had no idea about the unspoken rules of champagne tours."

Franck's eyes softened and he bit his lip. "Sorry. Of course you didn't. I guess I'm more tired than I realize." Our eyes remained locked for several beats. "Do you accept my apology?" he asked.

I sighed. "*Oui.* I'll apologize to Jacqueline when I get a chance."

"Thank you," he said. "You may get a free pass because, you know—"

"I'm not French."

"Yes. It can come in handy sometimes. *On y va.* Let's go get some champagne before my family drains all the bottles in the cellar. Hopefully they're familiar here at Clos de la Chapelle with Burgundians and their drinking habits."

We trailed at the back of the gang as we made our way down into the cavernous main room of the Domaine. It was entirely made of stone like the outside of the building and the ceilings must have been at least fifteen feet high with massive wooden beams crisscrossing in a haphazard fashion.

There was a large seating area with couches and armchairs around a cluster of five overturned barrels, but judging by the number of mismatched chairs that had been added I imagined they had to scrounge them from all over the Domaine to seat Franck's family. Mémé beckoned us to a worn green brocade couch where she sat beside Michèle.

I sat down, and then Mémé and Michèle pulled Franck down between them. I ended up at one end of the couch with Mémé sitting next to me.

"Isn't this wonderful!" Mémé clapped her hands together. We have our Franckie back! Can you believe it Michèle?" she crowed.

"I barely can," Michèle said brushing Franck's hair—which had grown a bit shaggy in what I considered a very sexy way, during our past few months in Montreal—off his forehead. 'We weren't sure if you would ever come back to us *notre* Franckie," she said, sending an inscrutable look in my direction.

If only I could have set the right mood with all of my presents...Instead, I gratefully accepted a flute of champagne from one of the Domaine's employees and listened to the red-sweater lady's explanation of this particular vintage. Seeing as I'd turned down the tour, I could at least be attentive to her spiel. Besides, when I wasn't frazzled with the combination of exhaustion and coffee, this was the sort of thing that I normally found fascinating.

When she gave us the signal that we could at last taste our champagne by saying *bon dégustation* I took a sip. It danced on my tongue. By god it was exactly what I needed, even though I hadn't realized it. I held up the flute in front of me. Visually, it was a work of art with tiny bubbles no bigger than pinpricks streaming upwards. The bubbles were fine and lovely, and the taste of the Chardonnay and Pinot Noir grapes came through with absolutely no acidity. It was perfectly balanced, vivacious, and tasted like a sparkle of mist in the sunlight that casts rainbows.

The woman said something about it being extra-brut, but I just knew it tasted like nirvana.

"Mmmmmmm." Everyone around us was moaning their appreciation and licking their lips. The woman stared with a slightly cowed expression at the flutes that emptied around the room, one after the other after the other.

"You were certainly thirsty!" she exclaimed.

Everyone nodded and laughed. "We're Burgundian!" Franck's uncle Jacques cried out. "We're always thirsty."

A second flute of champagne was served—rosé this time—and the laughter and the volume of the chatter grew louder and louder. Things became a little blurry after that, and the champagne bubbles seemed to rise in my soul and make everything seem wonderful.

I was floating, no longer feeling guilty at how much everyone had missed Franck, and no longer worried about the presents left in Montréal. Everything was hilarious and my flute kept being refilled. Each sip of champagne tasted better than the last.

Eventually, even through my champagne fog, I noticed that Mémé had her arms firmly around Franck's neck and was weeping. Michèle was doing the same thing on his other side. I reached across Mémé and tapped Franck's leg. "What?" I mouthed.

He just shrugged and smiled beatifically on his weeping family, clearly accepting this as par for the course.

"You cannot leave us again!" Mémé was making a wet patch on his sweater. "I will die before you return."

"Mémé," Franck said, stroking her hand. "That's exactly what you said when I left the first time, and yet here you are!"

"It's a miracle!" Mémé whispered. "We can't count on that happening twice."

"You seem quite robust to me." Franck rubbed circles on her back.

"But she's not!" Michèle protested. "We all thought she would die too." Fat tears rolled down her cheeks. I was too befuddled by this scene unfolding in front of me and the champagne in my blood to do anything but stare, slack jawed.

As an Anglo-Canadian brought up in a culture of stoicism, such indulgent displays of emotion were unthinkable. Even at funerals back home, people tended to exert every ounce of willpower to keep themselves together. Michèle and Mémé were completely, shamelessly, falling apart before my eyes, as well as carrying out blatant emotional blackmail.

Again, I had the familiar sensation of wanting to crawl under a table when I was around the pure French-ness of Franck's family. Part of me loved it, and part of me found it terrifying.

I glanced over at the barrels which now were covered by empty champagne bottles. I couldn't crawl under a barrel, and even if I did, I would probably fall asleep under there, which would not be the polite thing to do at all.

Maybe it was better to bite the bullet now and confront the unspoken issue before we got back to Burgundy.

"I feel guilty," I said to Mémé. "Taking him away from you."

Instead of protesting that there was no need for me to feel this way, both Michèle and Mémé nodded. "You should!" Mémé wailed.

"Um..."

"She doesn't mean that a bad way," Franck said.

But how could that be meant in a *good* way?

"We want you two to be together," Michèle explained. "We

know Franck is happy with you, but we don't want you to take him so far away."

I was stumped. "Well...I can't think of an immediate solution for that...not right now anyway..."

I looked over to Stéphanie, who was laughing with two uncles and three of her cousins, trying to telegraph my need for rescue.

Our eyes connected, and she nodded briskly. She got up and came over to me. "Laura's my friend," she said. "And we need to catch up. I'll be borrowing her for a while."

Franck looked up and whispered *merci* to Stéphanie.

I got up with alacrity, which was shocking given that I'd lost count of the flutes of champagne I'd imbibed.

Mémé and Michèle didn't pause for a second in their weeping and lamenting.

"Thank you for rescuing me," I said to Steph. "That was quite a scene over there."

Steph raised her eyebrows. "You think *that's* a scene?"

"It's not?"

"You have no idea." Steph cleared off a space on the other couch for me, unceremoniously ordering her cousin Léonard to shove off. She sat down in a chair beside me. "That's nothing," she said. "You should have seen them when Franck left to join you in Montréal. It was way worse."

"How is that even possible?"

"Both Mémé and my mother collapsed on the floor of Charles de Gaulle."

"No!" I gasped.

Uncle Jean nodded. "It's true. I as there. People were calling for a doctor."

"But *you're* a doctor."

"Yes, but I knew they were just being dramatic."

"You weren't worried about them...you know, medically?"

He shook his head. "I figured they'd get up eventually once they got the hysterics out of their systems. They feed off each other, you know."

"And they were united in their efforts to make Franck feel

bad," Stephanie added, with some asperity.

"Did they stay there for long?" I tried to picture the scene. "On the ground, I mean? It's filthy."

"André and I started walking off with Emmanuel-Marie and once they no longer had an audience—" He shrugged.

I glanced over at the trio again. "I wonder how long they'll be like this." The specter of the whole vacation filled with their wailing and gnashing of the teeth loomed in front of me.

"I suspect they'll be over the worst of it by tonight," Jean said.

I laughed. "Is that your clinical opinion?"

Jean just smiled. "*Bien sûr.*"

"But brace yourself as you get closer to your departure," Stéphanie warned. "It's going to start all over again."

"But it's not like Montréal is the *moon.*"

Stéph's quarter Uncle Bouffenoir leaned forward on the couch. "It might as well be," he said. "You have to understand for us here in Burgundy, Laura, we don't generally travel far."

"But Montréal is only six and a half hours away by plane! For goodness sakes, I have to take a five-hour plane ride just to get from my home in Canada to my university."

Then, it hit me. Growing up in Canada, I had become blasé about travel and distances without realizing it. My points of reference meant nothing in France. Here, you could be in Paris in the morning, Champagne in the afternoon, and Burgundy by early evening. Of course Montréal seemed like the moon.

"Ah!" Uncle Bouffenoir said. "I see it's sinking in now."

I nodded. "It's a bit depressing."

"Nothing a flute of champagne can't cure," Jean quipped, and got up to get a fresh flute for everyone.

chapter six

By the time our convoy pulled up in front of Franck's house in Villers-la-Faye I was delirious with...well, I hardly knew with what anymore. I'd gone beyond exhaustion and was now in a new realm of existence—the culmination of travel plus seven espressos plus six flutes of champagne.

Driving into Villers-la-Faye in Jean's van I tried to freeze the moment when I first caught sight of the spire of Villers' church in the distance. I had been looking forward to this solemn moment of homecoming with emotion, but now everything felt far too surreal to take seriously.

Everything both inside and outside me was blurred around the edges. When I opened my mouth to talk or moved my arm it felt as though I was moving through gelatin.

I stood on the rue de chaux and looked up at Franck's house—to the roofline where his attic bedroom was tucked under the eaves. All I could think was that within the next fifteen minutes or so I would be able to crawl into his bed. Had I ever craved anything quite so much? I doubted it.

I was carried with the stream of family into Michèle and André's courtyard. *Bed, bed, bed, bed* was beating a demanding tattoo in my mind, but I found myself being pivoted into the stone barn that was usually used to store old furniture and a thousand different treasures.

Despair washed over me when I saw the space had been cleared out, and filled with massive tables, beautifully set with bright red tablecloths, crystal wine glasses, and festive holiday plates.

"It's your welcome back dinner!" Renée swung me around. "Isn't it magnificent?"

I couldn't deny that. The barn *was* magnificent. I'd always thought so. The soaring ceilings, dry stacked rock walls, and huge wooden rafters were not dissimilar from the space we'd just been in for the champagne tasting.

Now that the detritus had been cleared away, I saw that the floor was made up of huge marble flagstones from the local quarries. It was chilly, but as all the family crowded in, I knew it would quickly warm up with body heat, just like it used to warm up thanks to all the livestock that lived there when Michèle was a little girl. The faint aroma of hay still hung in the air.

I was hauled to the far end of the table, which must have been set for over twenty people, where Franck and I had designated places, rather like the king and queen.

"Franck is officially home!" Mémé shouted and led everyone in a rousing *ban bourgignon.*

The mirage of Franck's bed was fading quickly, replaced by alarm. How could I possibly stay awake for a Burgundian meal, which often lasted upwards of seven hours? It was physically impossible.

Normally there was nothing I adored more, but with the way I was feeling…no matter how much sheer will I applied to the task of staying awake, there was just no way. While I appreciated the festivity and effort put into this, the meal stretched in front of me like climbing Mount Everest without oxygen. None of them knew, because few of them, if any, had ever experienced trans-Atlantic jetlag.

A glass of kir was thrust in my hand. Franck must have managed to free himself from the grips of his family for a few moments because suddenly he was beside me, and I felt his hand supporting my back. "Are you all right?" he asked, his voice concerned.

"No," I admitted, leaning on him so hard he had to stagger backwards before regaining his balance. "I mean, this is incredible. So lovely, but I just don't think I can physically do it justice. I'm going to fall asleep before the entrée is even served."

Franck studied my face. "You don't look quite right."

"Logical. I feel very far from right. I want to *not* be tired. Obviously. But I know myself and when I hit the jetlag wall, I go down. Hard."

"You should have slept more on the plane," Franck said, but he was tracing tiny circles on the back of my neck that felt so divine, so I just gave him a look.

"Ah. I forgot. You were furious with me."

"That's true, but honestly I've just never been good at sleeping on planes. How are you not fading?"

He bit his lip. "I slept all the way between Champagne and here."

I groaned. "You bastard. They kept asking me questions and poking me awake."

"I'm sorry," he said. "I'll make it up to you."

"Fine. I'll do my best, but from this point onwards I'm no longer responsible for what happens. Agreed?"

"Agreed. Take heart. I'll be sitting beside you—I'll prop you up if you fall asleep."

We sat down and drank our kir as André passed out baskets full of his wonderful *gougères*. Mémé told him ways to improve his recipe, of course, but that was par for the course.

Everyone was so loud and festive that I barely needed to say anything. I drank my delicious kir – that deep taste of blackcurrant liquor paired perfectly with the mineral dryness of the local white *aligoté* wine. How I had missed a proper Burgundian kir. I sat back in my chair and tried to take it in. My eyelids were drifting shut. Surely, I could take it all in with just my ears? My eyelids were so heavy. They just needed a little rest and then I'd be good to go.

It was the sound of a vineyard tractor chugging up the street that woke me.

I squinted, taking a moment to remember where I was and even who I was. My sleep had been a black hole, and I remembered no dreams, not even any moments of rising to anything close to consciousness.

The jaunty pirate wallpaper on the wall made me sit up. Wait...how did I get from the barn up to Franck's room? I'd fallen asleep at the table. Regret overcame me. I had missed that wonderful welcome back dinner! I reached out my arm and patted the other side of the bed. Empty. Where was Franck? Had he slept at all? What time was it anyway?

I studied the gray patch of sky through the skylight above the bed. The winter sky was dark and overcast—not very helpful for telling the time. For all I knew, it could be nine o'clock in the morning or three o'clock in the afternoon. I hoped I hadn't slept away my first day in France. That would be such a waste.

I stretched. I did feel much better for sleeping. Just then, the church bell from across the street began to chime. I froze as I counted the number of rings...eight...nine...ten. It was ten o'clock in the morning. I never slept in this late.

I needed to go downstairs and have a shower to wash off the travel grime. I dug my bathrobe out of my suitcase which, I noticed now, had been thoughtfully arranged at the end of Franck's bed and zipped open. I threw it on, grabbed clean clothes to change into, and headed down the three flights of creaky wooden stairs. As I neared the bottom, I heard the rumble of voices. Was all the family still here? Wait...was the dinner still ongoing even now? It wasn't unheard of in Burgundy.

I really wished I could see Franck before opening the door at the bottom of the stairs directly into the kitchen. A quick debrief as to what I was walking into would be useful. Maybe, I realized as an afterthought, I should be wearing something besides my dressing gown.

I took a deep breath and opened the door. Oh god. If only I could rewind that.

The only family I saw were Michèle, André, Mémé, Stéphanie and Emmanuel-Marie who was curled up like a contented baby fox in Franck's lap. This had to mean the dinner had ended.

The kitchen was full, however, with our friends. There was Olivier drinking a coffee beside Franck. Victor leaned against the kitchen counter, taking up a lot of space with his impressive size. Sandrine was there, and Martial, and Isabelle, and as soon as Martial exclaimed "Laura!" they all began to cheer and raised their hands in yet another spontaneous *ban bourignon.*

As overwhelmed as I felt, I grinned. It was incredible to see them all again, even though I was stinky and dressed in a ratty bathrobe. If they didn't mind, I guess I would try not to. Still, this was not exactly how I'd imagined our reunions.

I gave the round of *bises* to everyone and nobody seemed to visibly recoil at my breath, even though my mouth felt like the bottom of a birdcage.

"Can I get you a coffee Laura?" André asked.

A huge French bowl of coffee? That sounded like heaven. "*Oui*, I would love that," I said. "But first, I may just hop into the shower…you know, all the travel."

"*Bien sûr*!" he said and then called out for Michèle. Franck was already busy regaling his friends with a description of the thickness of ice that formed inside our bedroom's windows the year before, and everyone was completely spellbound.

I thought of asking exactly what had happened the night before, and how I managed to get upstairs, undressed, and into bed without even waking up, but I figured that could wait until after I was clean.

Michèle took my arm and guided me into the bathroom, showing me the fluffy towels and nice new bar of Savon de Marseille she had prepared for my arrival.

"Thank you so much," I said. "There's nothing that feels as good as a shower after a long trip."

"I can imagine," she said. "Franck woke up early and took his before I was even downstairs. It's all yours. Now, I want to go hear the end of Franck's story!" She closed the door behind her.

It niggled me that Franck had woken up and didn't wake me

up too. We only had two weeks here in France, and he must have known that I wanted to be up and showered and ready to enjoy the day like he did. He seemed to be enjoying himself without me, recounting his tales to an enthralled audience.

I jumped into the shower, taking a moment to sniff the delectable smelling shampoo and body gel. The French bath products always seemed to smell better than those back home. These ones were mint-scented and the tingly, sharp smell was exactly what I needed to finish waking me up.

As I lathered myself and began to feel more human, I reconsidered my initial, astringent, reaction to Franck not waking me. He deserved the benefit of the doubt. It was normal that he wanted some time alone with his family and friends after so long. I had no right to be churlish about that after he had left his home and family so that we could be together.

He'd probably let me sleep in because he knew how tired I was. That was an act of love and consideration, and I had to stop being selfish. I was bigger than that. Our couple was bigger than that. This time in France was legitimately more about him than me, so I would reconcile myself with taking the back seat. He needed this, and I loved him.

By the time I emerged from the shower, feeling about a thousand times cleaner and more amendable—my teeth freshly brushed with peppermint toothpaste, my body freshly clean and moisturized with delicious smelling lotion, my hair still wet and squeaky impeccable. Now I was ready to sit down, drink my coffee, and visit with everyone.

I walked back into an empty kitchen.

Michèle and Mémé came in just then from the garden with freshly cut bunches of bay leaves in their hands as I stood there, bewildered.

"Where is everyone?" I asked.

"Michèle kicked them out," Mémé laughed. "There wasn't room to turn around in here, and we need to make lunch."

"But...where did they go?" I asked, feeling abandoned.

"They moved over to Olivier's house," Michèle said. "Do you want your coffee before you go over there?"

Michèle and Mémé probably didn't want me hanging around when they tried to make lunch any more than Franck's friends. "I'll just head over there. I was wondering if I could throw my dirty clothes in the washing machine before I go though?"

Michèle put down her bay leaves. "I'll wash those."

I hesitated. They were really disgusting, and I didn't think it fair to give anyone else the job of handling them. "Honestly, I can do it myself. I don't mind."

"Just let her have them," Mémé said. "Michèle doesn't like anyone messing with her washing machine. Even me."

"Oh," I said. "All right then. Sorry for…well…sorry." I handed over the pile of clothes in my arms, feeling unaccountably embarrassed.

"They'll be nice and clean when they get back to you," Michèle said. I knew this much was true. Michèle was nothing if not a rigorous cleaner.

"All right then," I said. "I'll be off."

"Yes, yes, that's for the best," Mémé said. "We have some cooking to do. We're making Franck's favorite."

"Oh? What is it?" I ran through Franck's favorites in my head. Pig's feet. Veal kidneys, *andouillette* made of pig's intestines. I gagged a little.

"It's a surprise!" Michèle said.

And that, quite clearly, was my signal to leave.

I let myself out the kitchen door into the gravel courtyard. The tall barn doors where we had been seated the night before were now closed. Fog swirled in the air and the church bell chimed out eleven times. There it was—that magic of Burgundy that made me feel as though I was suspended in time.

I let myself out the wooden gates onto the street. A man in his work blues emerged from the village boulangerie across the street with three baguettes under his arm. He nodded his head and said *bonjour* before heading up the hill beside the church.

I stopped in the street and wrapped my arms around my torso. I was back here, in France, with Franck.

At so many times that had seemed like such an impossible

dream. The chilled morning, the dreaminess of the fog, the slight tang of limestone in the air from the freshly turned vineyards surrounding us, the old church looming in front of me, the lunch being concocted for us in Franck's kitchen—delicious or not time would tell—our friends hanging out at Olivier's place...all of it.

I had doubted I would be able to experience this magic again, yet here I was. I took a few moments just to savor the wonder and gratitude. It was miraculous to be back here, and I couldn't let pettiness overshadow that.

With this resolution, I walked up the massive raw stone steps of Olivier's house beside the boulangerie, a smile on my face. Inside was the life that I could just as easily have lost to me if things hadn't gone our way.

I opened the door without knocking and the crowd, which seemed to have increased by several people since Michèle's kitchen, turned and stared at me.

"*Me voilà*!" I announced. "Here I am!". Olivier began to cheer and the whole crowd joined in, then someone started singing yet another rollicking *ban bourgignon* and everyone joined in that as well. There was no doubt, I was definitely back in Burgundy.

"Laura!" Olivier came over and kissed me again. "What can I get you?"

"A coffee would be amazing."

"Ah...that's more like it," he said. "Still love your coffee, *hein*?"

"Always."

The coffee maker was always on an Olivier's house, and we went over there together. He took an espresso cup off the rack on his counter, but I stilled him with a touch to his arm. "How about a bowl?"

He laughed. "Right. How could I think otherwise?"

"To be fair," I said. "I haven't even had one today yet."

"Fair play," he said, and then took down a chipped painted pottery bowl from Brittany with his name written in calligraphy on the front. He filled it with pitch-black, steaming, heavenly nectar.

"Nice bowl."

"My parents went to Quimper on vacation about ten years ago. You'd be hard pressed to find a French person who doesn't have one of these in their kitchens."

He passed it over and I blew Olivier a kiss. "Thank you *mon ami*. You're a savior, as usual."

"There is no thank you between friends," he said. "We're just so glad to have you both back. The good-byes are going to be hard."

I laughed. "We just got here. Let's not think about that yet."

He grinned. "Fine," he said. "You're right, but us French are genetically predisposed to melancholy, you know. Besides, we're not used to our friends jetting around all over the world."

"Well, across the Atlantic anyway. I'll give you that."

"To us, it feels like across the world."

I nodded. "You're right," I said. "I guess it does."

"Come." He waved at me. "Sit."

He led me through the crowd and sat me in the worn leather armchair beside the roaring fireplace. Beside me, Franck held court on the couch, flanked by Martial, Stéphanie and her boyfriend Jerome, and the massive Victor.

The bowl of coffee burned my hands, but it felt divine. I took a sip. *Ah*. Olivier always made coffee so strong it could wake up the dead in the village cemetery above us on Mont Saint Victor.

Once the caffeine hit my system, I started to pay attention to what Franck was saying. It was dawning on me that everyone was casting me bemused glances during pauses in Franck's story.

"I came home to the terrible smell of burned peas," Franck was saying, and the audience leaned forward, hanging on his every word.

"Now, let me describe to you Laura's version of split pea soup, which is a traditional dish in Québec by the way, but *not* the way she makes it."

Oh God no. Not the pea soup story.

The audience erupted with laughter, even Olivier, who leaned against the wall...the traitor. I forced a smile. I was left with no choice but to be a good sport. Besides, if I looked at it objectively, it was a pretty funny story.

Franck recounted the whole tale of how my attempts at pea soup resulted in an irredeemably burned pot and a solid dome of congealed peas that had to be thrown out the back door into the snow below. It was not my finest culinary moment.

Some of Franck's friends, a few of who I didn't even recognize, were sitting cross-legged on the floor gazing at him in much the same way I watched Mr. Roger's on TV when I was four years old. When he got to the punchline—we'd found the mound of pea soup in the same place when the snow melted in May—they burst into gales of laughter. He had them in the palm of his hand.

Once the laughter had died down, I nudged Franck, who was still grinning. "Hey, how exactly did I get into bed last night?"

But instead of answering me in a quieter voice like I had asked my question in, Franck raised his. "That's right! I didn't tell everyone how Laura fell asleep with a *gougère* half-eaten in her mouth last night!"

"You don't need to tell everyone," I hissed. "You can just tell me."

But the crowd was already begging for the story, and Franck patted my knee. "It's too good not to share."

"Then shouldn't I hear it first?"

But by then Franck had already launched into his tale, starting in Montréal, of how he'd forgotten the presents and how cold it had been outside, but nothing compared to how icy I'd been on the plane. I sat back with my coffee, peering peevishly over the rim. I didn't need to hear this part, I'd lived it.

Finally, after many random tangents, Franck got to the part where I was sitting at the head of the dinner table in the barn and started to snore. I was apparently asleep even though I was still sitting straight up in my chair, with a glass of kir in one hand and a half eaten *gougère* sticking out of my mouth. He certainly painted a vivid picture.

"I tried to wake her up, but it was like she was in a coma," he said. "So I had no choice but to carry her upstairs and put her into bed."

"But that's three flights of stairs!" Victor exclaimed. Most of his friends had played in Franck's bedroom when they were kids, on rainy days when it was too wet to make forts on the Mont Saint Victor.

"I know," Franck said. "And there was no waking her up, so she was an absolute dead weight. She didn't even flicker an eyelid."

Everyone was greatly amused by this, but Franck didn't leave it there. He launched into a detailed explanation of the language politics in Québec.

Whenever I tried to correct him or moderate his comments when he got things wrong, I got the feeling from Franck as well as that of the crowd that my interjections were unwelcome. I gave up. This was clearly The Franck Show, and I was just getting in the way.

Whenever I had daydreamed about this vacation to France, I hadn't imagined this. I expected it would be mostly about Franck. I was fine with that; it was only fair. Still, I'd never expected that I would be cast not so much as Franck's girlfriend, but as some sort of comedic sidekick.

chapter seven

Lunch was delicious with no animal feet or innards, which I considered a win. Almost as soon as we sat down at the table, however, with Franck's parents, Mémé, Franck's little brother Emmanuel-Marie, Stéphanie and Jerome, Franck dove back into his stories of all the times I'd made a fool of myself.

Over the entrée of Mémé's soft and fluffy quiche Lorraine, Franck recounted how I'd slipped on the ice in front of the student union building and careened on my bum almost all the way down Metcalfe street until I caught myself on a lamppost near the bottom. He didn't, however, mention my sprained ankle, bruised tailbone, and massive hematoma on my hip and thigh.

Over the *blanquette de veau* (one of Franck's favorites I happened to love) he told the sorry tale of when there was a small meningitis outbreak at the University. My hypochondria kicked in at about midnight one night and I made us spend the entire night at the Montreal General ER.

By the time cheese had been devoured—an entire round of Cîteaux and a Délice de Pommard, creamy and covered with a crust of ground mustard seeds, and Mémé's deep, dark chocolate mousse and handmade *tuiles* biscuits – light as air and shaped on a rolling pin into the form of a roof tile in the South of France—arrived on the table Franck had launched into a new story.

Even the satisfaction of the mousse melting silkily on my tongue didn't remove my exasperation at Franck's embellished retelling of the time I got stuck up to my waist in a snowdrift on my way to school and had to be hauled out by a bunch of guys from a nearby Frat house. When had I suddenly become the butt of every joke?

After espresso, Stephanie and Jerome were leaving because they were preparing dinner for us a Jerome's house in Savigny-les-Beaune, and Franck suggested that we go upstairs for a quick nap.

I agreed. Franck might have a "nap" on his mind, but he was in for a surprise.

We climbed the three sets of crooked, wooden stairs until we reached Franck's attic room. He gathered me in his arms and began kissing me. "Finally," he murmured in my ear. "I've been wanting to do this all day."

I pushed him away. "Really? Well, guess what? You're the only one."

His eyes grew wide. "Is it the presents again? I don't know how many more times I can apologize for—"

"It's not that," I smacked him on the shoulder. "Do you realize that I've been the butt of your jokes since I woke up this morning?"

"Jokes?"

"I mean your 'stories'." I made air quotes with my fingers. All of your tales about Montréal—a few of which were exaggerated, by the way—feature me as the idiot."

"But...I just talked about the cold and the city and—"

"And my pea soup and me sliding down Metcalfe and getting stuck in a snowbank."

Franck tilted his head. "Come on," he said. "The pea soup story is too good not to share."

I sighed. It *was* a good story, but it was also humiliating, especially amongst Franck's family of amazing cooks. I was still trying to live down the time I had served them grape Jell-O at the end of my exchange year, much to their disgust. "I think that story on its own would be fine, or any of them, really. It's just that they're coming like machine gun fire—one after the other after the other."

"Really?" Franck said, and I could tell from his expression that his bewilderment was sincere.

"How could you not realize that?"

He shrugged.

"*Men*," I exhaled noisily and plonked myself down on the edge of Franck's bed.

"Are you sure?"

"Rewind and consider your stories from my perspective."

I also had words to say about his sudden need to grandstand, which was completely unlike Franck's normal behavior. He wasn't like that with his friends before I'd left, and he was never like that in Montréal. Where had it come from?

He reached for my hand. "I'm sorry. I'm just so happy to be home again and it's fun to have stories to tell instead of, you know, 'I went up to Dijon this afternoon'."

I understood that. From the perspective of his village, what Franck had done was quite unique. Most village kids ended up living in Villers or one of the neighboring villages, or maybe Beaune or Dijon. Paris was even a bit of a stretch. So what if he wanted to show off a bit? Didn't we all at some point?

"I get it." I squeezed his hand. "And I really don't mind the stories, even some of them where I look like an idiot. It's just not fun for me when they're *all* like that."

"I'll be paying attention to that from now on in, *promis*." He sat down beside me, then leaned over and gave me a kiss, then another, then another. "Now what was it about this 'nap'?" This time he used air quotes. "I'm not feeling very sleepy."

"With all that talking? I was certain you would be exhausted."

He tickled me. "*Coquine*."

I evaded his fingers and pushed him back against the bed, mock serious. "Jetlag is a very serious matter. With the time difference if we fell asleep now, we probably wouldn't wake up until tomorrow."

"That would be very unwise."

"Hazardous to our health, even," I said between kisses.

"Besides, I have to make myself forgiven," Franck sighed against my ear, his hands busy, divesting me of my jeans. "Properly forgiven."

"Yes," I said. "You have a lot of work to do."

"Then let's get to it."

The next day we went down to the wonderful boulangerie in Nuits-Saint-Georges to pick up pastries for dessert. Mémé had ordered them especially, but her, André, and Michèle were too busy cooking lunch to go down and pick them up themselves.

When Franck asked me to go, I was torn. I wanted nothing more than a drive through the vineyards, but at the same time Nuits-Saint-Georges was the home of two of my host families from my exchange year in Burgundy.

Of the two, I was definitely closer to my first family—the Beauprés—but things had ended badly at the end of my exchange year when I had chosen Franck over them. It got to the point where they considered packing me back home to Canada early.

I never regretted that decision, but I did regret the hurt it had caused. I wanted to call the Beauprés now I was back in Burgundy, but I just didn't know how to be with them now, knowing how much they'd disapproved of Franck. The whole thing filled my chest with prickly awkwardness.

Emmanuel-Marie decided to come with us to Nuits-Saint-Georges at the last moment, and he distracted me on the ride down by telling me all about a recent school field trip to a local violin maker who owned a bunch of goats.

Franck whipped through the vineyards towards Chaux, through the village, and then down the winding hill into Nuits-Saint-Georges. The familiar vineyards and the belltower of the Nuits' main church was nestled down in the valley. My bedroom with my third host family had been under the roof, right beside that belltower, and the booming bells became the cadence of my life for a time.

We found a parking spot on the main street and I surveyed the terrain before getting out of the car—it wasn't like me to be so furtive. I gripped onto Emmanuel-Marie's tiny hand. The last thing I wanted was for him to get into an accident on my watch.

We went into the bakery, and the tiny bell above the door jingled. I let out a long breath I hadn't realized I'd been holding. It was crowded with people—this boulangerie was *always* crowded with people—but nobody I knew.

I relaxed and breathed in the heady scent of freshly baked bread. Emmanuel-Marie and I admired the gorgeous lines of glossily glazed chocolate, café, and vanilla éclairs lined up in neat rows, along with showier pastries such as *les réligieuses* with all their frilly cream, and delicate flaky layers of the *millefeuilles.* It was every bit as breathtaking as walking into an artist's gallery, and it boggled my mind that *patissiers* all over France produced this beauty and deliciousness every day.

Emmanuel-Marie began tugging on Franck's jacket. "Can I choose a pastry?"

Franck frowned down at him. "It'll ruin your appetite, then Mémé will have my head."

"No she won't! She's missed you so much. There's no way she'll get mad at you."

"You won't feel sick?"

Emmanuel-Marie looked affronted. "I'm big now. I can eat *so much.*"

Franck grinned and ruffled his brother's hair. "All right, what do you want?"

"A Paris-Brest!" Emmanuel-Marie pointed at a circular cream filled concoction in the case.

"You sure?" I asked. "That's pretty big."

Emmanuel-Marie licked his lips. "Oh, I'm sure." It was fascinating to see the geneses of a true Burgundian *gourmand.*

"How about you Laura?"

France was no place for moderation. What a waste that would be. "A café éclair," I said, with a grin.

"I think I'll join you," he said.

Franck was served at the counter and I helped him carry all of our packages, including Mémé's order, plus a few fresh baguettes for good measure.

We trundled out of the store, and Emmanuel-Marie sunk his tiny baby teeth into the donut shaped Paris-Brest. Cream came gushing out the side and plopped onto his navy jacket.

Uh oh. Michèle was fastidious about such things.

Franck frowned. "Now we're in for it." He grabbed some Kleenex from his pocket and began dabbing at his little brother's jacket while Emmanuel-Marie munched happily away, unbothered.

While I was waiting, I sunk my front teeth into my éclair. The soft *chou* pastry gave way to the silky coffee cream filling. Like all French pastries, it wasn't too sweet, just deeply flavorful. How I'd missed this. We were almost back to the car and I was feeling triumphant. I'd slipped in and out of Nuits-Saint-Georges incognito and was eating a delicious pastry to boot. What could be better?

"Laura? Is that you?" My mouth still stuffed with éclair, I turned slowly. That sounded just like—

There stood Madame Beaupré in front of me, impossibly chic in a pale blue wool coat that matched her eyes, leather boots, and her blond hair back in a chignon.

I chewed and swallowed as quickly as I could, but I was sure it didn't look particularly elegant. I wiped my mouth. "Bonjour!" I exclaimed.

She leaned forward and gave me *les bises*. Her familiar perfume made my eyes prick with tears. I missed her. It also brought a wave of guilt. No matter what my reasons had been, I knew the Beauprés felt I'd abandoned them and their family at the end of the year.

"You're back!" she exclaimed. "And you didn't call us!"

"We just arrived two days ago." Franck came to the rescue. "And we're still recovering from the trip, not to mention being smothered by my family!"

She turned to Franck, her sculpted eyebrows raised. "Bonjour," she said.

"I'm Franck," he said. "Bonjour. You must be Madame Beaupré. Laura has told me so much about you."

Madame Beaupré's smile looked a bit more forced now, but then she caught sight of Emmanuel-Marie leaning against his big brother, munching on his pastry and licking his fingers. Her eyes widened. She had always loved children.

She leaned down to talk to him. "Bonjour."

"Bonjour." Emmanuel-Marie thrust out one small and very sticky hand.

Madame Beaupré shook it without hesitation. "And who are you?"

"My name is Emmanuel-Marie," he said. Madame Beaupré cast me a questioning look.

"This is Franck's little brother" I explained. "They're twenty years apart."

"He's adorable," she said, but before either Franck or I could answer, Emmanuel-Marie said, "Merci." We all laughed. I was so grateful he'd decided to tag along.

"How long are you here for?" she asked.

"We fly back to Montréal on January second," I said. "It's going to go so fast."

"Well, you both must come to lunch. I insist. Everyone will want to see you."

I both dreaded and looked forward to that. "That would be wonderful, but maybe after Christmas?"

"My family is keeping us quite busy, I'm afraid!" Franck said, charm incarnate.

"Of course," she agreed. "How about the day after Christmas?"

I raised my eyebrows at Franck. He was more informed about our social schedule than me.

"*Parfait*," he said smoothly. "That would be delightful. I look forward to it with impatience." He could be so smooth when he wanted.

"Wonderful!" she said. "We'll expect you at noon."

"I can't wait," I said. "Give my love to the whole family in the meantime."

"Of course, and good-bye Emmanuel-Marie," she said.

Emmanuel-Marie smiled and nodded, like a king receiving his due adulation. "*Au revoir*," he said. "*Et bonne journée.*" Wow. Franck wasn't the only one who could be smooth.

She laughed with delight, waved at him, and walked away. We all climbed back into the car. I let out a gusty breath. "Thank you Emmanuel-Marie," I said.

"For what?" he asked.

"For being so cute."

"Oh that!" He wiped his sticky hands down the front of his jacket. "It's nothing."

chapter eight

The days were going by too fast. I wanted to hit a pause button so I could draw things out longer.

Christmas was in two days' time, but it felt as though we had just arrived. Every day had been a parade of delicious food—a massive raclette dinner at Martial and Isabelle's house, a suckling pig at Renée's, a cabbage stuffed with delectable sausage stuffing at Victor's—and incredible, rare bottles of local wine. Nobody could host quite like the Burgundians. Nevertheless, I was aware of a background flutter of panic—there were so many people to spend time with and so little time.

Finally, after lunch on the day before Christmas Eve day, I realized that we still hadn't bought any presents for Franck's family to replace the ones Franck had left behind.

"We still have no presents," I said to Franck, after a delicious lunch of stuffed tomatoes that Michèle and André had made at the height of tomato season in September and frozen for us to eat over Christmas. They were filled with a juicy mix of sausage meat and onions, parsley, and garlic which created amazing juice, all soaked up by the accompanying basmati rice. We were sipping our espressos and our thoughts had naturally turned to what the afternoon would hold.

Franck tapped the table. "You're right."

"*Cadeaux! Cadeaux! Cadeaux*!" Emmanuel-Marie chanted as he banged his spoon on the table for emphasis.

"We don't need any presents," Michèle said.

Emmanuel-Marie's round brown eyes turned to his mother.

"I need presents!"

"Well, maybe Emmanuel-Marie," Michèle conceded. "But not André or me or Steph or Mémé."

"Really?" Franck said, quite ready, I got the impression, to go along with his mother's suggestion. "*Aie*!" he yelped and clutched his calf. I'd kicked it under the table. "What was that for?"

"Sorry," I said. "Accident, but I do think we should head to Beaune this afternoon."

"Fine." He looked up at me accusingly while he rubbed his leg.

"Can I come? Can I come?" Emmanuel-Marie got out of his chair and began jumping up and down.

"No, *pétit frère*." Franck reached out and tousled his blond hair. "If you're with us than we can't buy your present."

"Why not?"

"Because then it wouldn't be a surprise."

"Oh." This obviously made sense in his five-year-old mind.

"I'll go upstairs and grab my jacket and my bag," I said, getting up from my chair.

"Al right," Franck said. "But I'm just going to have a bit more coffee before we leave."

"You have to tell me everything about Christmas in Canada, Franck," Mémé leaned forward and clasped his hand.

I sighed as I made my way upstairs. We may not be headed into Beaune for a while yet.

It was impossible not to be in a Christmas mood in Beaune. The entire town was decorated with fresh greens and red and gold ribbons. Bundled up vendors were literally roasting chestnuts as per the iconic Christmas song on open fires in front of the market *halles*. Their scent of toasty nuttiness permeated the crisp December air. Beaune—a perfectly preserved medieval town—was picturesque at the best of times, but never more so than during the holidays.

After Franck had given Mémé a full and comic description of Christmas in Canada the year before at my house, Olivier and Martial had dropped by for a quick visit. It was three o'clock by the time we got out of the car on Place Carnot and began strolling around, hand in hand. This was the exact type of moment I had daydreamed about.

"I guess we only need to find something for Emmanuel-Marie," Franck said.

I shook my head. "No. We need to get something for everybody. Mémé, your parents, Emmanuel-Marie, Stéphanie, and Jerome."

"But my mother said—"

"I heard, but I'm going to buy gifts for them all the same."

"They really wouldn't mind."

"I would."

"Is this about the presents I left in Montréal?"

I still felt a faint pang when I thought of those carefully selected presents sitting on our bed in our freezing bedroom back on the rue Coloniale, but I was mainly over it.

"I've forgiven that...or almost, anyway. It's just that you're their son, but I'm a guest at your parents' house. This is my first Christmas with them. Remember how last year when you arrived at my house, you brought the wine glasses from Burgundy and how that went over so well?"

"But that was different. I was worried your father was going to murder me for moving in with his daughter, so it was as much an act of self-preservation as anything else."

I shrugged. "Maybe, but it helped smooth the way, didn't it?"

Franck nodded. "I suppose, but I didn't speak the same language as them. I needed some kind of peace offering."

"Still, it was important to you to feel thoughtful."

This gave Franck pause. At my house he'd gone over and above to be the perfect house guest. He made sure he washed every last dish there was to wash, he unloaded the dishwasher, he insisted on doing his own laundry, and he ensured he was up before my mother every morning so he could make her a fresh pot of coffee. That, more than anything, had conquered her heart completely. It had been of vital importance for him to be thoughtful, so surely he could understand why I wanted to do the same.

"Ah," he said. "I see now."

I nodded. "We have our work cut out for us. Where do you think we should start?"

Franck pointed at a brand-new storefront across from us on the Place Carnot with the name "Atheneum" carved into the marble frontage. "That just opened," he said. "Stéphanie and my parents have told me it's incredible. It has a huge selection of books and toys and so much else."

"*On y va.*"

Three hours later Franck and I were sitting on a café terrace off the Place des Halles, not far from one of the chestnut vendors. Chimney smoke and the tang of spilled wine mixed with the starchy scent of the roasted chestnuts, and I was positively bursting with the Christmas spirit.

Night had fallen quite some time earlier, and now the town felt even more magical than before, if that was even possible. Tiny white Christmas lights were strung everywhere overhead in swooping canopies over all the pedestrian streets. It created rippling waves of light above us, and it was breathtaking. The ancient façade of Beaune's famous *hospice* belltower was lit up. Laughter and the notes of Tino Rossi's classic "Pétit Papa Noel" drifted out from inside the café.

At our feet were bags of beautifully wrapped presents—the French had a gift for exquisite packaging. I thought I'd done a decent job with the presents I'd prepared in Montréal, but they were nothing compared to the curls of golden and silver ribbon artfully arranged over glittery paper of the same hue.

Franck's family had been right, Atheneum was a glorious store filled with everything we needed—three new books and a wooden train set for Emmanuel-Marie, a cashmere throw for Mémé, who was always cold, a necklace for Michèle and another for Steph, a bottle of wine for Jerome, and a book on Impressionist paintings for André.

I had no room left in me for anything besides relief and Christmas cheer. We were over our jetlag. Franck still told the pea soup story and the sliding down Metcalfe one, but he'd lightened his touch. He told stories about his own blunders as well. Now I could just sit back and enjoy the magic of it all.

"Franck?" A voice came from behind us. "Is that you?"

A pétite blond woman, adorably attired in a camel duffel coat and a cozy red scarf that set off her fair hair, came towards our table.

I recognized her immediately. Juliette. Franck's ex-girlfriend. The one who had broken his heart. I could suddenly relate to Ava's loathing of a girl in a camel duffle coat.

I'd met Juliette only once before—by accident in Dijon a month or two after meeting Franck. Now, just like then, I felt all wrong beside her. Too curvy, too Canadian, too strident…all those feelings came rushing back.

She leaned down and gave Franck a kiss on each cheek, lingering rather too long for my liking. She smiled at me and reached out her hand. No *bises*. That was a blatant way of saying she had her reservations about me the interloper.

"So, you've returned to Villers?" she asked, including only Franck in her beaming smile.

"*Oui*," Franck said. "We have. Do you remember my girlfriend, Laura?"

Love surged through my chest. He wasn't going along with Juliette's attempts to make me feel invisible, thank god.

Juliette's mouth tightened and she nodded at me. "Of course."

"We've been here about a week," he said. He pointed down at the bags at our feet. "We've just finished Christmas shopping for my family."

"How are they?" She smiled. "I miss them *so* much."

Cow.

"They're well."

"And Emmanuel-Marie? He must be getting so big by now. I remember when he was born. That was such a special time, do you remember?"

I knew exactly what Juliette was doing—reminding me that she'd been around for more important moments than me. It was there in the flutter of her eyelashes and the way her entire body swayed towards my boyfriend.

"Emmanuel-Marie is wonderful. It was hard being so far away from him."

"*Bien sûr* it must be. Even though I'm at school in Paris now I just can't imagine being far away from Villers-la-Faye. I mean, Villers is where we're from, *n'est-ce pas*? Our roots run deep." She flicked a triumphant glance at me before turning back to Franck and saying soulfully, "I think I would wither away if I couldn't get back for a quick weekend."

Franck's face looked troubled. I knew at many times during our year together he'd felt torn between our life in Montréal and his life back in France. I hated how guilty that made me feel, and I hated even more the knowledge that if he was still with Juliette, he would never have to feel that way.

"I need to hear all about Montréal," Juliette leaned closer to him. "I've been hearing about nothing but you since I got back from the holidays. You're the conquering hero! My parents are always like "Franck, this" and "Franck, that", recounting all your stories about Canada they heard through the village grapevine. You've become the talk of the village."

Franck couldn't hide the flattered gleam in his eyes. This hero-worship was hard for me to comprehend, because in my world people living abroad for a year or more was a common event. People moved and traveled all the time—besides the First Nations people, the rest of us were basically immigrants to Canada.

"When can I see you?" Juliette asked. "I want to hear *every-*

thing." I didn't miss that she used the French singular form of "you", meaning Franck only, instead of the plural form which would have included me.

"Well…Laura and I have a busy schedule," Franck began.

Bless him.

"But my parents have been wanting to see you too," she said, with a small pout. "Could you not make just a tiny bit of time for us?"

Franck looked at me again and I struggled to keep my face as bland as possible. I might be a wretched tangle of anger and insecurity inside, but I'd be damned if I was going to give Juliette the satisfaction of knowing that. "I'm sure we can," he said. "But it will have to be after Christmas."

Her eyes darted back and forth between Franck and me. "*Fabuleux*," she declared, but for a flash she looked seriously put out, which gave me a spurt of satisfaction. "I'll be in touch."

With that, she was off, swinging her slender hips as she walked back across the *place des halles. Damn these camel duffel coat girls.*

So many words burbled to the surface, but I swallowed them down. They hurt, like jagged glass in my throat, but I didn't want to say anything until I had a private moment to unravel my thoughts.

"We'll just go for a quick *apéritif* or something after Christmas," Franck said, shrugging in apology.

The whole scenario sounded ghastly. I just couldn't picture myself at Juliette's house, sitting bodkin between Franck and his ex-girlfriend, with her parents for an audience. *Non merci.* "I didn't get the impression I was included in that invitation," I said, despite my best efforts at restraint.

"Of course you were!"

"She used '*tu*' instead of '*vous*'," I pointed out. "I'm good enough at French now to catch things like that."

"I'm sure that was just a slip of the tongue."

Huh. She wishes. "Not so sure" I gathered the bags around me. I was too restless now to sit still any longer. Besides, I'd finished my drink and we were due at Stephanie's for dinner.

"Wait." Franck placed his hand on my arm. "Are you mad that I accepted the invitation?"

I reminded myself that he had accepted the lunch invitation for the Beauprés even though they'd been hostile about him in the past. "I'm not thrilled about it," I admitted, and stood up. "But I'll survive." We had to get walking before my restraint slipped completely.

"I'll be sure to keep it short for us."

Even with Franck's best intentions, I knew once he launched into his tall tales of Canada, all hope of a quick visit would be lost. I bit my tongue though. It felt as though merely opening my mouth was courting danger. There was just too much turmoil inside me.

"I would feel bad refusing," Franck explained. "And if it was just Juliette asking, I probably would. It's just that I was extremely close with her parents and they were nothing but kind to me. They took me on every one of their vacations and allowed me to go to places like Spain and Portugal that I never would have seen otherwise."

That thought made me a bit nauseous, but it was mixed with guilt. "Don't mind me," I said. "Just promise me not to tell the pea soup story."

The belltower rang seven o'clock. "*Zut*, but it's my favorite one." He swept me up in a kiss under the lights that left me breathless. "I love that story because I love you and how much fun you bring to my life. You know you have nothing to worry about with Juliette, right?"

"Right." My doubts faded but didn't disappear completely. For the moment, though, all I could do was kiss him back.

chapter nine

It was Christmas Eve Day, and we just finished a quick lunch in Villers-la-Faye and were packed into the car headed for Montbard, where we would be having dinner at Jean and Jacqueline's house and celebrating Christmas Eve. The only people missing were Stéphanie and Jerome, who were celebrating it with Jerome's family in Savigny.

En route, we were visiting an old monastery close to Montbard called l'Abbaye de Fontenay that had recently gained UNESCO world heritage status. Emmanuel-Marie was deeply underwhelmed by this program.

"It's beautiful," Franck assured me as we drove past frosty hills where white cows stood, looking bored and cold. Their massive heads were wreathed with clouds of condensation from their breath.

"You don't have to convince me," I whispered back. Emmanuel-Marie, who sat on the other side of Franck, watched us, his eyes round. "You know I love old things."

"I don't want to go," Emmanuel-Marie said. "It's boring."

Emmanuel-Marie was dragged on cultural excursions frequently, and I could hardly blame him for being fed-up.

"But the film Cyrano de Bérgerac was filmed there two years ago," Franck told Emmanuel-Marie. "You know, the one with Gérard Depardieu."

Emmanuel-Marie raised his thin blond brows. "I only watch cartoons," he said, disdainfully.

Franck nodded. "I see."

"It's very, very ancient," Franck tried again. "It dates back to the twelfth century, when there were knights and kings."

Emmanuel-Marie shrugged his tiny shoulders, unimpressed.

"It's the oldest preserved Cistercian Abbey in the world."

Good God, what was Franck thinking?

Emmanuel-Marie merely sighed and turned his gaze out the window. "I'd rather watch cartoons."

I tried to think back if I would've been similarly unimpressed at Emmanuel-Marie's age. Most likely. I would've chosen an episode of Scooby-Do over an ancient monastery.

"It was a valiant attempt." I squeezed Franck's thigh.

Franck waved his hand, unbothered. "It shows he's a normal child I suppose, which is a good thing."

"What Emmanuel-Marie falls short of in enthusiasm, I promise I can more than make up for. You know me—I love this sort of thing."

We'd seen Cyrano De Bérgerac at our favorite arthouse cinema, the Cinéma de Paris on Saint Catherine's Street in Montréal, a few months previously. Fontenay Abbey played such a central role in the movie that it was practically a main character.

"I always loved that about you." Franck leaned over and kissed my earlobe. I had to remind myself that his little brother was sharing the backseat with us, and his parents were in the front seats. "Juliette was always bored by these sorts of things."

Juliette? Franck never made reference to Juliette. Why now? Should I just take what he said as a compliment, or should I think deeper about whether Juliette was suddenly on Franck's mind? A worm-like bitterness squirmed in my stomach. I hated feeling jealous and uncertain. Generally speaking, Franck—even though he could often drive me bonkers—rarely made me feel either of those things, in stark contrast to a few of my ex-boyfriends.

This wasn't the place, or the time, to get into it. Franck had started tickling Emmanuel-Marie, so I gazed out the window at the tiny stone villages we were passing.

Everything about the Burgundian countryside—the undulating hills, the slow-moving white cows, the worn stone of the villages—felt so gentle, so benign. It changed softly with the seasons, but it always had a calmness that was a balm to my soul.

I came from a place of jagged cliffs and wild ocean storms and trees so huge it took three or four people with the arms outstretched to encircle their trunks. It was a place where the air smelled of brine and bears and cougars wandered into town on a regular basis.

To be here in Burgundy, which always felt so safe, and thinking of Juliette, who made me feel insecure, was jarring. Being back here with Franck frequently felt like a dream. Sometimes I worried that it would disappear like one too. If that happened, not only Franck, but this whole part of my life, would be lost to me. It was an appalling thought. My logical mind knew I was probably making something out of nothing...still, Franck and Juliette had gone out several years longer than Franck and I had been together. Maybe she hadn't been able to imagine it ending either.

André pulled the car into a gravel parking spot, and I shook my head. *Enough*. I was not going to let myself obsess over Juliette and wreck my first Christmas in France with Franck.

I hopped out of the car and saw a gorgeous, golden stone chapel in front of us. Perfect. This visit would be an ideal distraction.

Seconds later, Jean and Jacqueline's minivan rolled up beside us. A flurry of kissing began. Mémé had returned to Montbard the previous afternoon when we'd been in Beaune, to help with the Réveillon dinner tonight. The way everyone was talking about it, it promised to be spectacular. Mémé immediately claimed Franck as hers as we made our way into the entrance of the abbey.

Jean appeared beside me. "I will tell you everything about Fontenay," he said. "I know the entire history by heart."

"Super!" I tried to sound enthusiastic. "My very own tour guide!" I adored Uncle Jean, but he talked at moved at about a third of the normal speed of most people. Patience had never been my strong suit at the best of times.

Mémé and Franck were off into the gardens, which were bare of flowers but beautifully structured and laid out. Mémé leaned heavily on Franck's arm and I watched as their figures grew smaller in the distance. Mémé was so incredibly special, and they loved each other so much. The good-byes were going to be nothing short of agony.

"Are you listening?" Jean asked me, as we stood in front of a rather beautiful, though worn, statue of the Virgin Mary holding baby Jesus.

"*Oui, oui*," I assured him, although my mind had indeed been elsewhere. "Of course. Fascinating."

"So, as I was saying, this lovely statue is called 'the Virgin of Fontenay'." He paused to gauge my reaction. Only when he determined I looked suitably impressed did he continue, "it is one of the finest examples of thirteenth century medieval sculpture in Burgundy. You see how it contrasts with the austere architecture of the rest of the Abbey?"

"I do."

"That anomaly alone shows the strength of Saint-Bernard's devotion to the Virgin Mary."

Who was Saint-Bernard? There were just so many Saints in Catholicism to keep track of, a veritable panoply, and I wasn't even Catholic to begin with. I didn't dare ask though, as we'd never catch up to the rest of them if Jean launched into that tangent.

"Ah! Let me tell you more about Saint-Bernard." Jean lifted his index finger, sooooooo slowly. "Because that is the crux of it all."

Too late.

It wasn't until at least an hour and a half later of my own private, slow-motion tour that I saw Franck's distant figure reappear across the gardens. Jean was exceedingly erudite, and he would have been a superb tour guide if only he would speed up by about ten times his actual speed.

"Why don't we go join them?" I pointed out the figures of Mémé and Franck, flanked, I could see now, by his parents and

Emmanuel-Marie. I could see from where I stood that Emmanuel-Marie was dragging his small feet.

"But I was just about to show you the cloisters," Jean protested.

"Wouldn't it be nice to see it all together?" I asked.

Jean frowned and rubbed his chin as he thought about this. Then he thought about it some more. In the meantime, I waved energetically in hopes Franck would come and rescue me. Please God let him get the message.

He waved back, and started to make his way over to us, leading everyone else in our direction. Uncle Jean was still pondering my question.

"Ah!" I said. "They're coming our way. Lovely."

Jean shook his head. "Mémé and Jacqueline will want to go too fast. They're too impatient.

I had a good idea of why they were so impatient, but by that time Franck and his entourage had joined us at the edge of the garden.

"So?" Jacqueline asked me. "What do you think?"

"It's absolutely beautiful," I said, in all honesty. The buildings were absolutely sublime in their stark, simple beauty.

"Isn't Jean an excellent tour guide?" she said. "So knowledgeable."

Yet, I couldn't help but notice that Jacqueline herself, even though Jean was her husband, wasn't availing herself of Jean's guide services. "The best," I said, and smiled with wide eyes at Franck, signaling 'rescue me!'. "But I feel guilty monopolizing him."

"That's true," Franck said, gently removing his arm from Mémé's, and reaching out and taking my hand. "I'm going to give Laura a private tour of the cloisters if you don't mind."

"But—!" protested Jean.

"No, no," Franck said. "You've given her such a wonderful tour already. I insist. The others could benefit greatly from your expertise. They deserve a turn."

Ignoring the reproachful looks being sent at him, he took me by the hand, and we dove into the cloisters. He didn't need to urge me to keep up.

We went around one corner, and then a second, then a third. It was stunning. Serene, uniform, peaceful, and bathed in a soft golden winter light.

"This place is incredible," I said as we finally slowed down. "It's a shame I don't have Jean here to explain it to me."

Franck turned to me with a grin and pulled me behind an arch between the pillars. "I can take you back to him if you like."

"Hmmm." I wrapped my arms around Franck. "I can't deprive the others."

He chuckled and leaned down to trap my mouth in a searing kiss.

I broke away after about a minute. "Won't the others be coming soon?"

Franck snorted. "You did just spend an hour and a half with Jean, didn't you? Trust me, they are not moving fast."

I'd only seen one other visitor besides Franck's family wandering the grounds and they had appeared to be on their way out, so Franck was probably right. We could be alone for a while. "You sacrificed me." I tried to swat Franck's shoulder, but he locked his arms around me, pressing me tightly against his chest.

"I did," he admitted. "I'm sorry. It's just Mémé hadn't seen me in almost twenty-four hours and it made Jean so darn happy—"

I bit his neck.

"Consider it a rite of passage." He was shaking with mirth. "An initiation, if you will. You're truly part of the family now."

"You bastard," I said, but lovingly. I kissed him again and for a long while we were lost in each other. It felt so heavenly to have him to myself for just a few minutes, at a time when we weren't both digesting massive meals of wonderful food and wine like a pair of boa constrictors on his bed.

Something about the crisp winter air and the pious surroundings woke a wildness in me, and I could sense Franck felt the same. His hands slid under my sweater, and mine under his, and things started to get rather frenzied.

"We can't here," I sighed.

"I can't help it," he whispered back, his words ragged. "I don't know if I can stop."

I felt the same, but I was aware that the rest of them could walk around the corner at any time. We were partially hidden by the pillars, but we would need a moment to...ah...straighten ourselves up.

"There has to be a place we can go," Franck said. "I want you so much Laura. Right now."

"Me too," I said. "But—"

Franck grabbed my hand and ducked in a doorway just a few feet away from where we were standing. It led into an incredible, cavernous room that a sign on the wall designated the 'chapter room', although I had no idea what that was.

The intersecting arches that made up the ceilings and the pillars were some of the most beautiful things I'd ever seen. "Wow," I murmured.

Franck located a particularly chunky pillar near the end of the room. "*Parfait*," he muttered, and whipped me around so my back was against it. The twelfth or thirteenth century stone—Jean could undoubtedly tell me which—was hard and unyielding against my spine, but it merely stoked my lust. We picked up exactly where we'd left off.

Ten minutes or so later, when things were reaching a critical juncture behind our pillar, a voice echoed from the far end of the room. "And this is the chapter room." Franck and I froze. It was unmistakably Jean's voice. "This space was one of the cruxes of Cistercian monastic life."

"Yes, yes, of course," Jacqueline said, but it sounded a bit like she was snapping at him.

"Do you know where it gets its unusual name?" Jean asked.

Nobody answered, although I could hear several pairs of footsteps as Franck and I frantically tried to straighten out our clothes. I smoothed down my hair with shaking fingers.

"Hmmm. Can't guess, can you? It's because every morning in this room the monks would read a chapter of the rule of Saint

Benedict and comment on it before the daily work was handed out to the monks." Maybe Jean didn't require a receptive audience to conduct his tour after all. Did he even notice? I wondered.

"Jean," Jacqueline said. "That's all written on this plaque here by the door."

Franck licked his fingers and tried to wipe something off my chin.

"What?" I mouthed at him.

He frowned. "I scratched your chin with my stubble." He kept his voice low so it couldn't be heard over Jean's intonations and the rustle and chatter of the rest of them.

"Yes, yes, this room is very nice," Jacqueline said. "But we should find the young lovebirds and get home. We have a meal waiting for us."

"But—" Jean protested, and Michèle echoed his sentiment. She liked to take her time in such places too, but preferably alone.

I jerked my head to where their voices were coming from with raised brows. *Should we show ourselves?*

"This is also where the monks would confess their mistakes," Jean said, as if he'd never heard Jacqueline.

I stifled a giggle. Franck stepped out from behind the column. "Ah! Bonjour," he said. "We're down here."

Everyone's heads swiveled in our direction. "Didn't you hear us?" Mémé demanded.

"No," Franck said. "Strange, *n'est-ce pas*? I suppose these arches make for some unique acoustics."

In the meantime, I skirted behind the columns to position myself a bit away from Franck. I gazed out the stained-glass window in one of the alcoves.

"Isn't it stunning?" I said loudly, adopting a particularly soulful tone of voice, as if I'd been marveling over the architecture all this time.

"Ah!" Jacqueline said. "We're all here then. We should be heading back to the house."

"What's the rush?" Michèle asked.

"We need to eat dinner before we go to midnight mass at the nunnery chapel.

"What nunnery?" I asked Franck, who had joined me, his hand resting lightly on my lower back. This was turning out to be a piously themed day...well, except for our interlude behind the pillar.

I could tell from the horizontal lines that had appeared in Franck's forehead that this nunnery business was news to him too. "There's an active nunnery on the hill by Jean and Jacqueline's house. She's very close with the nuns there. I didn't know this was planned though."

"But we never talked about midnight mass," Michèle protested. After years of being extremely religious Franck's parents had started to question the church and, more to the point, Jacqueline's fervent praying and hanging out with nuns. It was to the point if that Jacqueline had mentioned the midnight mass at the nunnery, I doubted Michèle and André would have accepted the Réveillon dinner invitation in the first place. They'd been duped.

"Didn't we?" Jacqueline said, airily. "Well, I suppose I thought it went without saying. It's unthinkable *not* to attend midnight mass to celebrate the birth of our Jesus Christ."

If Jacqueline only knew how pagan my family back in Canada were...

"But it's such a long service Jacqueline," André said. "We have to drive back. Emmanuel-Marie won't be able to—"

"Now, now." Mémé patted André's arm. "You'll all come. If at a certain point you need to leave, they will understand."

Jacqueline furrowed her brow at this. It was clear she didn't take kindly to the idea of anyone from her entourage departing the mass early and, I imagined, coming across than less than devout in the eyes of the nuns. Jacqueline was an extremely generous person as well as a formidable host, but the religion thing was part of the package.

Franck had told me that she hadn't been very religious when she was younger. Ironically, she'd always rebelled against the family tradition of attending midnight mass on Christmas Eve.

That all changed, though, one year when she was volunteering as a nurse in Lourdes—the iconic Catholic pilgrimage site where the Virgin Mary was believed to have appeared to a peasant girl on several occasions. Jacqueline had found herself alone in one of the many chapels and had undergone a powerful religious conversion in there.

I always hungered for more details on exactly what had transpired, but even Jacqueline was vague about it. She'd befriended her nunnery friends shortly after and had become more and more devout ever since.

This was a squabble that had nothing to do with me, and I was relieved to remain just an observer. Franck wisely held back too.

Mémé was always trying to be the peacekeeper, and I knew that Michèle and André resented it. This had the potential to turn into a rather interesting Réveillon dinner.

chapter ten

We made our way back to the cars and drove back to Jacqueline and Jean's house perched up above the Burgundy canal. All the way, Michèle maintained an energetic tirade about Jacqueline's excessive attachment to the nuns who, Michèle said, were hiding from the world.

When we got inside the foyer of the house, Mémé bustled us in and took off our coats off and pushed us up the stairs where the kitchen and the main living area were located.

The place was decorated for Christmas with a medium-size Christmas tree, but also a heck of a lot of crosses and icons of the Virgin Mary.

I'd been to Franck's aunt and uncle's country house in a village called Montigny, which was actually more of a chateau. Jean had inherited it from his family. That's where I was invited to Mémé's gargantuan eightieth birthday party with Franck and the rest of the family. It had lasted the entire weekend and it had been glorious.

Their house here in Montbard was altogether less grand, but still roomy and cozy, with deep leather couches and a crackling fireplace. There were also delectable smells wafting out from where I assumed the kitchen must be behind a swinging door.

Jacqueline emerged with a huge woven basket of *gougères* in her arms. My mouth began watering as I smelled the aroma of butter mixed with the scent of the melted Emmenthal cheese Mémé always used in her recipe.

"Jean!" Jacqueline hollered. "Our guests our here! You must

come and serve the kir."

Jean came dawdling out of the kitchen with a benign smile on his face. Maybe Jacqueline was the more religious one in their couple, but it was Jean who had the countenance of a Saint.

"Ah!" He clapped his hands together, but at Jean-speed. "Welcome. We can't have you without a kir, now can we? Laura, have you tasted kir before?"

I could sense another history lesson coming, so I answered quickly, "Yes, yes, I love it."

"And do you know the origins of the drink? It all began—"

"Yes!" André broke in, which was extremely out of character for him, but he must have needed a kir as badly as I did. "We explained it all to her." I snuck him a smile and he smiled back.

"Pour Jean!" Jacqueline commanded. "Do not let our guests go thirsty. That would be very unburgundian of us."

She clearly knew the right thing to say, because within the next ten minutes we all had garnet flutes of bubbling kir in our hands—Jean had mixed the *crème de cassis* with Burgundy Crémant, as per tradition for bigger celebrations such as Christmas Eve.

After a lovely *apértif* during which Franck always had a hand or a finger touching me somehow, Jacqueline commanded us to take our seats at the table. I was beside André and Mémé and Franck was across from us. Mémé, however, was up and down constantly to the kitchen, as was Jacqueline.

"Can I help?" I called over to Jacqueline as she began to bring artistically arranged plates of foie gras out of the kitchen along with baskets of toasted brioche rounds.

She turned to me, aghast. "*Jamais*! You're the guest!" Right, I'd forgotten how seriously the French took hosting. Still, I felt badly that here I was sitting and Mémé, at eighty-two years old, was hopping up and down from the table to serve us.

I raised my eyebrows in question to Franck and he nodded slightly to let me know that this was how things were done.

I inspected my plate. Luckily, I had already learned during

my first Christmas in France that I adored foie gras. It was one of the traditional entrées of celebratory french meals. When it was first described to me as fattened goose liver I'd entertained some rather serious doubts, but that was before I'd taken my first heavenly bite of the silky, delicately flavored indulgence.

The thin slice of foie gras had a massive black round item embedded in its center. This was new.

"Is that a truffle?" I asked Franck, nodding down to my plate.

He licked his lips. "It certainly is."

"It's huge!" Back home truffles were doled out at snobby restaurants as dried flakes or truffle infused oil in everything, but never had I seen such a blatant chunk of truffle presented so simply and generously.

"Burgundy specializes in this type of truffle," Franck said. "They're rare and very coveted."

Jacqueline and Mémé sat down, and after a prayer during which Michèle rolled her eyes so far back in her head I worried they might get lost back there, we were instructed to begin with many wished "*Bon Appétits*".

I took my first forkful—a bit of foie gras, a bit of truffle, and a few flakes of *fleur de sel* that had been sprinkled on top. I scraped this on a lightly toasted brioche circle. In my mouth the combination was soft and crunchy with the meat flavor of the foie gras and the sweet, nutty taste of the truffle dancing in exquisite harmony.

I sat back in my chair. "Wow," I murmured at my plate. This was precisely one of those times where I felt like I'd never truly known just how delicious food could be before coming to France.

"*C'est bon?*" Jean asked.

"*C'est délicieux.*"

"Don't forget the wine." He pointed at the honey tinted liquid in my cut crystal wine glass in front of me. "It's a very old *Sauternes*. I picked it out to drink with the foie gras."

"Wonderful," I breathed and took a sip as Jean watched me. It was sweet and cold and went perfectly with the other flavors.

"Oh," I breathed, "It's perfect."

"Everything has to be perfect," Jean said. "It's your first Christmas with us, after all."

Jean was a dear man, despite the interminable history lessons. A magnanimous glow radiated upwards from my stomach. All of Franck's family was lovely. Christmas in France was lovely. Franck was lovely. This was perfection.

"Thank you." I smiled at Jean. "That means more to me than you can know."

It was midnight and Franck and I were surrounded by nuns. I had gone to a Catholic school my first year in Burgundy, so I wasn't as perplexed by nuns as I used to be, but I still found them vaguely unsettling.

Franck and the rest of his family, on the other hand, acted as though a flock of nuns in their black robes with white wimples covering their hair and massive wooden crosses around their necks, was a routine thing.

They nuns were all half-chanting and half-singing something in Latin…or maybe it was Greek. Honestly, I didn't know either well enough to tell the difference.

We were somewhere in a tiny stone nunnery chapel in the hills above Montbard—a world away from Montréal and our apartment on Coloniale Avenue. All of us non-nun people were seated against the side wall on a rather cold and extremely hard wooden bench.

A priest had arrived at the beginning of the mass in the most glittery, ornate regalia I'd ever seen, complete with a high embroidered headdress. He greeted everyone then disappeared behind an equally embellished curtain at the front of the chapel. So far, he hadn't reappeared.

When I whispered to Franck about this, he whispered back that this particular nunnery was some form of orthodox

Catholicism, so the priest led the mass from behind the curtain, because his form was too holy for female eyes. I couldn't help but roll my eyes at that misogynist sounding claptrap. Besides, the priest, for all his fancy outfit, must have been one hundred and ten years old if he was a day, and had a long, scraggly beard stained with tobacco. Hardly the stuff of temptation.

I could tell Michèle was similarly unimpressed. As expected, Emmanuel-Marie had fallen into a deep sleep and was snoring lightly with his head on Michèle's knee. Michèle was stroking his hair and pointedly ignoring the reproachful looks that came from Jacqueline. Michèle, for her part, kept nudging André in the ribs and hissing derisive commentary to him.

Mémé, clearly used to staying above the fray when it came to quarrels between her daughters, smiled benignly and cast many adoring looks over at Franck.

"How long is this going to last?" I whispered to Franck. The cloying smoke of the incense was clogging my throat.

He shrugged. "No idea. Long, I would imagine."

I sat back against the bumpy rock wall and coughed as quietly as I could manage. The whole ceremony was interesting from a cultural perspective, but we'd just finished a Pantagruelesque meal of stuffed capons, a gargantuan cheese platter, and Mémé's legendary *bûche de Noel*. It went without saying that the wines were extraordinary. The started out amazing and finished with sublime. Even though I'd bolted several espressos at the end of the massive Réveillon meal, I wanted nothing more than to crawl into bed. We still had that drive ahead of us, after all.

Wait. Something was happening behind the curtains. The nuns and Jacqueline all held their hands up in the air, like some sort of evangelical revivalist event, and began waving them back and forth singing "Hosanna".

The priest burst out from behind the curtain, his face glowing with pride. He lifted up his grizzled hand. "Hosanna!" he shouted three times, and the nuns all shouted back. Franck nudged me. I looked up to see he was standing, as was everyone else except me and Emmanuel-Marie. How did they know when it was time to do that sort of thing?

I stood up and lifted my hands above my head, copying the others. I said "Hosanna" a few times, but I just couldn't muster up the enthusiasm of the others. I still wasn't quite sold on the whole God thing, let alone the Catholic thing, let alone the Orthodox Catholic thing in a nunnery. My inner feminist was irked by the fact that a man had to come to do the important stuff.

I looked over at the priest again. He was looking exceedingly impressed with himself, as though he alone was responsible for the birth of baby Jesus.

Thought-provoking, but I still wasn't convinced.

The next morning, Emmanuel-Marie woke us up by leaping on our bed. "Wake up! Wake up!" He bounced. "*C'est Noel! Le Père Noel est venu!*".

I rolled over and groaned. The church bells rang out seven times. We'd maybe had three hours of sleep or so by the time we got out of the monastery and drove back to Villers. I had no idea how André managed to stay awake at the wheel.

Seven o'clock actually wasn't too bad considering the ungodly hour I used to wake up on Christmas mornings when I was little—my earliest I think was four o'clock in the morning.

"My slipper is full of bon-bons!" he shrieked. "And there's a new present for me under the tree!"

Ah, it was lovely to have a little one around at Christmas.

I'd found out my first year here that there was no such thing as Christmas stockings in France. Instead, children left out their slippers for *Le Père Noel* who filled them up with shiny-wrapped chocolates and candies. It was definitely more cost-effective for Père Noel compared to all the little toys and things it took to stuff a stocking.

"That's so exciting!" Franck wrestled him into a hug. "Why

don't you go back down? We'll put our robes on and come down right away."

"You have to hurry." Emmanuel-Marie sat on Franck's chest and poked it. "I mean it."

Franck saluted him. "Aye captain."

"Promise?"

"*Promis.*"

When he scampered off Franck rolled over so we lay face to face. "*Joyeux Noel mon amour.*" He gave me a kiss.

"*Joyeux Noel,*" I whispered back and gave him one of my own.

It was incredible to be here, with Franck, waking up on Christmas morning in France. It was only our second Christmas together, yet we'd already created so many memories on this trip—so many wonderful laughs, so many amazing wines, so many shared moments with friends and Franck's family.

Even the less-than-magical moments like bumping into Juliette in Beaune, my lingering flashes of guilt, and the forgotten presents were things Franck and I were experiencing and figuring out together. Each one of them—the good and the bad and everything in between—was building our lexicon and history as a couple.

"Are you as tired as I am?" Franck asked.

"Probably." It had been one o'clock in the morning by the time the mass was over. Then we had to say *adieu* and *merci* to all the nuns as well as Jean and Jacqueline. We'd brought Mémé back to Villers with us and arrived in the village at three o'clock in the morning. "But it's Christmas."

Franck nodded. "You're right." He got out of bed and then walked to my side and pulled me up as well, then gathered me against him. "It's going to be a fun day."

Would it be the first of many? Sure, Franck and I had talked about the future, but it still felt as though there were so many things to work out. Time would tell, but I wished I could know.

Sadly, Père Noel hadn't left any chocolates in my slippers—there was probably an age limit for that—although I suspected I didn't need to worry about starving on Christmas day in Burgundy.

Once we'd made our way down to the kitchen, we saw that everyone but Stéphanie was already up. Mémé, in fact, was taking several fresh baguettes out of the oven. I'd bet Emmanuel-Marie hadn't needed to wake her up.

"Did you just make those?" I asked.

"Of course," she said. "I owned the *boulangerie* across the street, *tu sais*. Once a *boulangère*, always a *boulangère*."

"But...what time did you get up to get those ready?"

She laughed. "You mean what time did I go to sleep? The answer is I didn't really. I never sleep well anyway, so I figured I might as well bake fresh bread."

That was a new idea. Like everyone else, I'd had my bouts of insomnia, but it had never occurred to me to get up in the middle of the night and bake bread.

"Now!" Mémé said. "Who wants fresh *tartines* for breakfast?"

"*Moi! Moi! Moi*!" we all chimed in. It was truly amazing that we could fit anything into our stomachs after the previous night's meal, but perhaps the midnight mass had miraculously helped our digestion. My stomach was actually complaining of hunger.

Or, as Franck always reminded me when it came to eating or...more frequently...bedroom activities...*l'appétit vient en mangeant,* or "the appetite grows as you eat."

"But the presents!" Emmanuel-Marie protested as Stephanie opened the door from the upstairs to the kitchen. "We don't have time to eat! We have to open our presents."

"We need to wait until Jerome gets here." Stephanie rubbed her eyes and yawned. "We can't start opening presents without him.

"But why?" Emmanuel-Marie flung himself against André's legs. "It's not fair!"

I didn't blame him one bit for being frustrated. Delaying present opening would have driven me around the bend at his age.

We all sat down, even though Emmanuel-Marie was still grumbling. Mémé put the still-warm baguettes on the table with a package of salted butter from Brittany and some of Michèle and André's jam made from the wild peaches that grew at the end of the vineyard rows. I knew there would be tons of delicious food to come, but I always felt that restraint in France was a travesty.

Franck placed a steaming bowl of black coffee in front of me. I glanced outside the kitchen window, where frost clung to the stones of the barn outside and coated the bare branches of the twisted ivy vine. Round, red-breasted robins chattered as they hopped branch to branch. It was so cozy in the kitchen with the intoxicating smell of fresh bread and its uneven rock walls and all of Michèle's antiques and little knick-knacks she wedged in the spaces between the stones.

I cut myself a chunk of baguette, then sawed it in two. Steam wafted out the middle and brought with it the delicious scent of yeast and comfort. I slathered on the butter and the jam, then dipped the first slice in my coffee and took a dripping bite. It was delicious. Soft, coffee infused baguette, melted butter, and the fruity note of peach jam melted in my mouth.

Christmas Day in France was off to a good start.

chapter eleven

The presents didn't take a long time to open. There were two or three per person, and that was it. It dawned on me that all the gifts I had bought in Montréal to bring over may have been a bit over-the-top given the simple nature of the celebrations.

Jerome had arrived, and it felt nice to not be the only non-family member there. Our eyes would catch when Steph and Michèle butted heads or Michèle gave André a hard time or Mémé started in again on how she didn't know how she was going to survive if Franck left again. We'd share tiny, knowing smiles.

After showering and making ourselves presentable, it was time to take a seat at the table Michèle and Mémé had festively decorated for Christmas. The theme was red and green, with accents of gold in the candles and ribbons that ran through the elaborate tablescape.

Mémé had a special skill for folding napkins into all kinds of fancy shapes. She'd made swans for this special meal, alternating between red and green on each plate as you went around the table. There were four glasses at each place setting, excepting Emmanuel-Marie—a champagne flute, a white wine glass, a red wine glass, and a small, beautifully etched glass that caught my attention.

I held the one up at my place. "What's this one used for?" I asked Michèle.

"It's for the *digéstif*," she said. "It's the little drink we have after the meal to help with our digestion."

"This is such an exquisite little glass," I said. The intricate loops of etching on the crystal were not quite uniform, which made me think it was probably hand carved. "It looks like an antique."

"It is," Michèle said. "It was handed down to me from my paternal grandmother. She always told me they'd been handed down to her from her grandmother. I only have three left, but I knew you'd appreciate it."

I certainly did, but I also knew that Michèle would not appreciate me *breaking* it either, so I set it down gently on the tablecloth. "Thank you," I said. "They're just incredible."

"But I'm leaving them for Stéphanie," she added, with an arch of her eyebrow.

What? Surely she didn't think I'd been angling for them? "I'm sure she'll...I'm sure that she'll love them," I said, awkwardly stumbling over my words.

"I'm not." Michèle grimaced. "She'll probably break them all within a year, but she *is* my daughter."

I frowned. Did Michèle think I had been casing her house for things I wanted? How unpalatable. Changing the topic was the only thing to do. "Can I be of any help in the kitchen or bringing things to the table?"

She shook her head. "No, it'll be crowded in there for more than Mémé and me with all our bustling around. Neither of us like people underfoot."

I just nodded. It was probably wise to talk the least amount possible, otherwise I'd unwittingly find myself in more hot water.

Renée arrived at the table then—she was joining us for Christmas lunch. Her arrival was dramatic and majestic as usual. She worse a scarlet cape adorned with a sparkly green holly pin. We spent many minutes kissing and wishing each other a merry Christmas.

Franck came in from the kitchen and sat down beside me. "I tried to help, but Mémé started snapping her dishtowel at me to get me out."

"I just asked your Mom if I could help. She didn't have a

dishtowel to snap but she might have if she did."

"Are you ready for another Burgundian meal?" Franck patted his stomach.

"Always, but surely this one won't be as long as last night."

Franck started laughing and couldn't stop until I ground my heel down into his toes. "Oh," he gasped, half-pain, half-laughter. "My poor, innocent child of summer."

When finally Michèle and Mémé sat down, André poured the kir royales, and we toasted "Joyeux Noel" again and began to get merry.

This time the first course was paper thin slices of cold-smoked salmon with a pat of salted artisan butter and thick wedges of lemon. There was also a platter topped with raw oysters on the shell nestled on a bed of crushed ice.

Michèle, Emmanuel-Marie and I abstained from the oysters—if I was in this meal for the long-haul, eating something that I might or might not want to throw up would not be a wise move.

But the smoked salmon…yum. I had grown up on my Dad's fresh caught and home-smoked salmon, but this was an entirely different food. The briny ocean taste of the thin slices went perfectly with the soft baguette and the creamy butter that sparkled with chunks of sea salt from the North-Western coast of France.

We drank a bottle of Premier Cru Chablis with the seafood and the mineral taste of the chilled wine with the briny, buttery combination in my mouth was sent straight from the heavens.

How, I wondered for the umpteenth time, did the French do it? The combinations of simple flavors created something new entirely, and something that was just pure, unadulterated pleasure.

Renée sucked down a raw oyster and smacked her lips with satisfaction. "There's nothing like a good meal," she said. "If I can't eat and drink anymore. You might as well put me in the box and be done with it."

"Box?" I whispered to Franck.

"Casket," he whispered back.

Whereas Jacqueline's hallmark was an unabashed devotion to God and the nuns, her sister Renée's was an equally unabashed devotion to pleasure.

"I'm going to remember that."

We laughed and talked, and as we waited to digest and clear up the first course, I realized I truly felt like part of Franck's family.

I looked over the table to see Jerome's lean cheeks had taken on a greenish hue. Stéphanie had convinced him to try an oyster even though he'd never eaten one before and hadn't been particularly keen. Jerome worshiped Stephanie. He probably would've agreed to eat an owl pellet if she asked him too.

"How is that oyster sitting?" I asked Jerome.

He frowned. "You made the right choice." Beads of sweat were popping out on his forehead under his head of curls.

"I think I did." He was looking queasier by the second.

Steph glanced over at him. "You don't look good. But It can't be the oyster. You only ate one, and besides, they are so delicious. How can you possibly feel sick?"

Renée glanced at his face. "Oh!" She chortled. "Jerome's face reminds me of a New Year's lunch we had fifteen years ago with twenty guests. The oysters we served were off and by the end of the lunch all our flowerpots were full of vomit!"

Jerome sprung up from his chair with a violent clatter, his hand clapped over his mouth. "*Pardon*," he managed to yelp before dashing out of the room.

It was crystal clear where he was heading, and what he needed to do there.

"The oysters can't be bad!" Michèle said. "We bought them from the best man from the market."

Yet she had abstained, and I was triply glad I had too. Poor Jerome. He would surely have to leave after being sick and miss out on the rest of the festive meal. If he was anything like me, he would be rigid with mortification.

Jerome's departure didn't seem to put any sort of pall on the conversation or the drinking as we waited for the main course, which was a goose that Stéphanie had bought off her friends who had a farm in Echevronne.

"Oh no," I said. "Jerome is going to miss out on the goose."

"But why should he?" Renée looked astounded at such a preposterous idea.

I decided to point out the obvious. "He's sick."

Renée waved her hand in one of her trademark majestic gestures. "Poo! So what if the oyster comes back up? It will just leave more room for what's to come."

"I don't think he'll have much of an appetite."

"It will return," she said. "Just like his oyster did. There is no good reason to abandon a meal mid-way through."

"There has to be exceptions to that," I laughed.

"Well...," She cocked her head as she considered this. "Perhaps death, but you really couldn't be so ill-bred as to expect anyone to move your corpse until they're finished *their* meal, so technically you wouldn't actually be leaving the table."

We roared with laughter over this, everyone except Renée that was, as she obviously didn't see the humor in what she considered the common sense.

The goose was brought out of the kitchen, cooked to golden perfection with a fragrant crispy crust. Chestnut and sausage stuffing was bursting out of its rear. As we were all ooo'ing and ahhh'ing, Jerome returned, looking much refreshed. He took his place, rubbed his hands together, and licked his lips. "That looks delicious," he said. "I can't wait."

I sat there with my mouth hanging open at his resurrection. He had looked *terrible*.

"Better?" Steph asked him.

"Oh yes," he said. "And starving."

Renée let out a cry of victory. "Excellent! You see Laura, in Burgundy, meals are all about carrying on!"

And so we did. We carried on through the goose and stuffing, which was out of this world. I didn't think I'd ever eaten goose before, but it was perfumed and moist and made turkey look rather like an insipid cousin.

Then André brought us out more beautifully carved glasses of a much needed *trou normand* to help us digest before the cheese and dessert courses. This time it was apple sorbet with calvados poured over top and it went down to perfection.

We carried on through the huge platter of cheeses including and entire round from the nearby abbey of Cîteaux (made by the monks) and a massive Soumaintrain that was like an Époisses on steroids. It was stinky and scrumptious.

We carried on past the *bûche de Noel* that Mémé made so expertly – layers of *gateau de savoie* rolled with ganache and pastry cream filling—one coffee flavored and the other chocolate.

We carried on past the coffee and chocolates and mandarin oranges. I was feeling fuzzy and at one with the world, as well as so full I could feel every heartbeat behind my eyeballs.

Franck had his hand draped over my shoulder and was drawing lazy circles on the nape of my neck.

Renée leaned back in her chair and smiled benevolently at the table. "Now that," she announced to the room. "Was a worthwhile meal."

"Laura and I might go upstairs for a quick nap," Franck said, although from the electric feel of Franck's fingers against my skin I was fairly certain a nap wasn't what Franck had in mind. Even though I was stuffed, a long, indulgent meal had a way of awakening other appetites as well.

Renée winked at us. "You mean "*une sieste crapuleuse*?"

I knew what that meant—a "naughty nap". Even though it was true, heat rushed up my face at the idea that our…ahem…intentions were being discussed at the table. There was my Canadian puritan upbringing. Amazingly, France hadn't managed to beat it completely out of me yet.

"That's exactly it." Franck winked back at her. "Although I was *trying* to be subtle about it."

Renée poo-poo'd this. "Subtlety is overrated. *Une sieste crapuleuse* is one of the greatest pleasures on earth. There is no better way to cap a large, long indulgent meal."

Franck just nodded, a remarkable show of restraint, whereas my face throbbed with my blush.

"Make the most of your youth and your *siestes crapuleuses*, *mes cheris*," she said, "There's nothing so beautiful as being young and in love. Now with my Marcel gone, I can't have them anymore, and even in those past few years before he finally slipped away—"

She shook her head and clapped her hands together again. "Enough of such maudlin moanings. Seize the day! Go upstairs and have *une sieste crapuleuse* for all of us that can't."

I looked over at Jerome, who was shaking with suppressed laughter.

"We will do just that." Franck stood up, pulled me up as well, and dragged me out of the dining room. "*À tout à l'heure*!" he called over his shoulder as he pushed me into the staircase that led up to his bedroom.

My face was still burning when we got up there. Rain had begun to patter on his skylight, and it was undeniably inviting to hop into his cozy bed under the huge oak beams. "That was *mortifying*." I buried my face in his shirt.

Franck chuckled, walking backwards as he pulled me towards the bed, unbuttoning my top as he went. "Why?"

"They were all talking about us." I gestured toward the bed. "You know."

Franck kissed me as he slid my top off my shoulders and threw it aside. "So?"

"It's not something to discuss at the table!"

He kissed my collarbone and my breath caught in my throat. "It is in France."

"Oh my lord," I said, as he pushed me onto the mattress on my back. I arched my neck to give him better access for his gentle kisses. His lips were so gentle and warm that my embarrassment was rapidly fading. "I thought I was going to die."

"Let's check if you survived," he murmured, and that is the last thing we said in a while.

chapter twelve

The next day was our lunch with the Beauprés.

Unbelievably, after our *sieste* the day before, we had made it back and found Mémé preparing a massive round of escargots for dinner.

"Dinner?" I looked up at Franck, who was still holding my hand.

"Aren't you hungry?" he asked.

"No...not really." I surveyed my stomach, but the smell of the parsley garlic butter Mémé was stuffing the escargot shells with was enticing...maybe I could eat just a few... "but those smell good."

"Mémé's escargots are the stuff of legend."

"They certainly are," Mémé confirmed, without interrupting her workflow for a second.

Amazingly, I managed to eat a dozen, but I was put to shame by Renée and Jerome who both put away two dozen each.

So, despite skipping breakfast on what would be Boxing Day back home, but was just a normal day in France, I was not feeling particularly hungry to sit down to another meal in Nuits-Saint-Georges.

It wasn't just because of my lack of appetite that I wasn't feeling ready for the lunch. I missed the Beauprés. Part of me couldn't wait to see them again. They'd so quickly felt like an extension of my actual family, and I would never forget that. Since I chose Franck over the Ursus Club, however, things felt stilted.

I knew they didn't approve of me getting so serious about someone at such a young age. Their daughter Sophie, who was sent to a small town in Washington State on the same exchange as I was, was only a year younger than me. They never would have accepted such a thing from her. They saw me as their de facto daughter, and worried about me accordingly. It might have been easier if Franck had come from their more well-to-do circle of friends around Beaune and Nuits-Saint-Georges, but that wasn't the case.

André was an Xray technician, whereas the close friends of the Beauprés were the radiologists he worked for. As my French improved, I began to see that society in France was just as stratified as elsewhere, perhaps even more so.

The Beauprés were firmly members of the *bourgeoisie*, whereas Franck's parents were a bit of an anomaly—self-educated and extremely cultured members of the rural working class. They didn't quite belong amongst many of the winemakers in Villers-la-Faye either. Michèle and André weren't at all interested in issues of land ownership, wine politics, or soccer, but preferred classical music, literary fiction, and art instead.

"I think I should warn you," Franck said as he pulled on a nice navy cable knit sweater that I loved. "I got in a fight with the Beaupré's older son in Middle School."

Shit. He'd gotten in a fight with Antoine? "Over what?"

Franck shrugged. "Just kid stuff. I was part of the gang of village kids, with Olivier and Victor and the rest. We thought we were tough, although we didn't bother people if they didn't bother us. Victor and Antoine got into a thing though."

"What thing?" I asked.

"You don't need to hear all this."

"I think I do." I wanted to go in as prepared as I could be.

"Antoine was mocking Victor's lack of brand-named clothes."

"He did that?" I asked, shocked. The few times I'd met Antoine, who was already living in Grenoble with his girlfriend when I at with the Beauprés, he'd seemed perfectly nice.

"Yeah." Franck sat down on the edge of the bed to tie up his nice shoes. "He always came to school with all the latest brand-named sweaters and backpacks and everything—always neat as a pin with not a hair out of place."

Having met Antoine I could believe this. He was very perfectly put together all the time. "That doesn't surprise me."

"People like that," Franck said, staring into the middle distance. "You just want to mess then up a little bit, you know? Just to see if they're actually human after all."

Strangely, I understood that too. I'd always been repulsed by people who had too varnished a surface. "So you guys got in a fight because of that?"

Franck shook his head. "No, if it was just that we would have left him alone. We all knew if we got into it with him and his friends, who were carbon copies of one another, we would be the ones who would be blamed and punished. The teachers and the administration always preferred the kids who came from the bourgeoisie families, you know?"

I sat with the uncomfortable realization that I had been one of those kids, and that my family background had been working in my favor my whole life without me seeing it.

"They were the haves," Franck continued.

"And you guys were the have-nots?"

"Not really." Franck ran a hand through his hair "There were worse have-nots then us—the kids who lived in the apartment towers on the outskirts of Beaune, or the farm kids that didn't even have indoor plumbing in their houses."

I gasped a that, but Franck was so lost in his memories it didn't seem to register. "We didn't think of ourselves as the have-nots, but when we were side by side with Antoine and his friends, that was the way we felt."

"That makes sense."

"Like I said, we would have left them alone, but then Antoine and one of his friends started mocking Victor, asking if his parents were too poor to buy him any nice clothes."

"That's gross," I said.

Franck nodded, but I could tell his mind was in the past more than the present. "The thing was, Victor's parents *didn't* have a lot of money. What made it worse was the fact they'd been distracted because his older brother had died suddenly of stomach cancer."

I remembered hearing about this, and how Victor's brother had been diagnosed, and then died two weeks later. I'd seen his grave in the village cemetery on the top of Mont Saint Victor.

"The whole family was paralyzed with grief," Franck continued. "This whole village was, actually. Victor had grown so much, so fast, and his parents were so deep in grief that he was growing out of all of his clothes. It's true that his clothes were tattered, not the cleanest, and three sizes too small, but all of us were so worried about him and his family after losing his brother—nobody was thinking about clothes."

"Of course not," I murmured.

"To think that Antoine and his friends, who were always perfectly turned out and looked to us like they'd never endured hardship in their lives, were making fun of Victor..." Franck shook his head.

I could tell that his disbelief still lingered, even now. "What did you do?" I whispered, wishing at that moment that I could travel back in time and punch Antoine myself.

"We caught them after school one day before they walked home. We missed our bus for it. I took the first punch. I knocked Antoine to the ground and his nose started bleeding—I didn't break it though, and at the time I wasn't sure if I was relieved or angry about that. He curled into a ball and started blubbering—all talk but nothing to back it up, like all of his friends. Olivier and Victor took on the other ones. They all started crying and begging so it was over pretty quickly. They said they were going to tell on us, but by that point we didn't care. Victor needed to know, especially right then, that we had his back."

"Were you punished in the end?" I asked.

"Of course," Franck said. "Suspended for a week."

"Did you get in trouble with your parents?"

Franck shook his head, a smile on his lips. "No. My parents understood that we did what we had to do. In fact, the three of us got special treats all week—we were the village heroes for a while there. All sorts of anonymous people would drop delicious baking and treats off in front of our gates."

I laughed. "I love that."

"Yeah," Franck said. "Solidarity. We take care of our own. But you can see why, all these years later, lunch may be a bit awkward for me, especially if he's there."

I frowned, lowering myself down beside Franck on the bed. "You don't have to come you know. I hate to put you through that."

"Don't feel badly." He rubbed my thigh. "These people are important to you, so I just want it to go well. I'll be my most charming and diplomatic self, I promise you."

I sat there beside Franck, not knowing how to feel. This was a side to the Beauprés that made everything more complex. It was something I needed to know, but at the same time, didn't want to know.

With mixed feelings, I stood up and pulled him up after me. "Well, even if we can't do anything about this being awkward, at least we don't need to be late."

"I suppose you're right," he admitted.

So many memories came rushing back when Franck pulled up his Dad's car in front of the Beauprés white house in Nuits-Saint-Georges. I remembered arriving the first time, direct from Monsieur Beaupré's mother's country house in the countryside outside Paris. I'd been completely disoriented and barely understood a word of French.

They had made me feel instantly at home in their daughter's room and Julien, the younger brother, had welcome me like a sister. I remembered the mornings Monsieur Beaupré had taken me jogging in the vineyards just two streets over, showing me the amazing Cistercian Chateau, Clos de Vougeot and encouraging me to sneak over the stoned wall of the Romanée Conti vineyards with him and snack on a few of the world's most expensive grapes.

My months with them had been wonderful—the best possible introduction to France—but things changed when I met Franck. They didn't approve, I dug my heels in, and what was simple became complicated.

I still hadn't made peace with all that in my heart. I would choose Franck again, without question, but I still regretted that I had to make the choice at all.

Franck tugged my earlobe. "Where did you go?" We were standing on the front porch. I was holding a massive bouquet of roses we'd bought at the *fleuriste* on the way, and Franck held a beautiful bottle of Corton that Martial had gifted him in the past.

"I'm not sure, but I'm back now." I had to be the mediator here, breeze through and try to smooth any round edges that popped up. I'd been taught how to do this since I was little; I just needed to get my head in the game.

I knocked on the door and Madame Beaupré flung it open.

"*Ma Laura*!" she cried and embraced me warmly on each cheek. I was enveloped in Guerlain Shalimar and memories of how much I'd idolized her came flooding back. She was still the most elegant woman I'd ever met. "How we've missed you!"

When she finally let go, she smiled politely at Franck, but that spontaneous warmth she'd showered on me evaporated in an instant, replaced by…not so much antipathy as hesitation.

"*Bonjou*r." She stuck out her hand, as always adorned with beautiful and expensive rings.

"*Oui*." He nodded and leaned towards her and warmly gave her a *bises* on each cheek. He smiled his most winning smile. "Bonjour. Thank you so much for having us. Laura talks about you so often that I feel I know you already."

Madame Beaupré's shoulders dropped. I don't know what she'd been expecting with Franck, but certainly not a charm offensive.

We were ushered into the living room where Julien came

over and gave me a warm kiss, as did Sophie. Robert appeared, a furrow that I recognized well in his brow.

"Bonjour Laura," he said, giving me a kiss on each cheek, but not with the warmth he used to. He stuck his hand out to Franck. "Franck," he said. "Welcome to our home."

Franck shook it and then passed him over the bottle of wine. Robert's brows flew up when he read the label. I knew it would impress a connoisseur such as himself. "This is an excellent producer," he said. "Very hard to come by."

"I do love a good Corton," Franck said. "My friend Martial is related to the family, so I have an inside track."

Robert turned this over in his mind and nodded his head. I was certain Franck had scored a point. "Ah...well, lucky for us. Come sit."

Antoine came in the room just then, saying something to his mother as he walked through the door to where Robert had seated us. He stopped as he spotted Franck, his eyes widening like a deer spotting a cougar. If we'd been alone, I would have laughed.

It was abundantly clear to me that despite the fact Franck had grown up and was dressed in his nicest pair of jeans and a lovely cable knit blue sweater, Antoine recognized the boy who had punched him in the nose.

"Antoine," Robert did the introductions. "This is Laura's boyfriend, Franck."

Franck stood up and extended his hand for Antoine to shake, a smile on his lips that could be interpreted in a variety of ways, depending on what one knew about their shared history.

"*Bonjour*," Antoine said, and I could have sworn I saw his pupils dilate.

"We've met, actually," Franck said.

"Have we?" Antoine said airily.

"Yes, we went to *college* and *lycée* together. We were in the same grade."

Antoine squinted his eyes at Franck, but he wasn't fooling me. "Really...how strange...I don't remember you."

"I remember you," Franck said. "Maybe you remember my

friends Victor and Olivier? They were from Villers-la-Faye as well."

Antoine became suddenly transfixed by Madame Beaupré's arrangement of dried flowers to the left of the chimney. "Didn't they end of going to trade school? Didn't you as well?"

"They did, yes," Franck said. "But I continued on and got my master's in communications from the Sorbonne."

I knew that Antoine had gone to a less-than-prestigious but very pricy marketing school down South and was anything but an intellectual. He didn't have much to say after this. He sat down in the farthest armchair from Franck and started talking with Sophie.

After a lovely *apéritif* where Franck kept Monsieur and Madame Beaupré amused with stories of Canada, but none which featured my mishaps, we moved to the table.

Madame Beaupré's food was exquisite as usual—an entrée of delicious pumpkin soup with crème fraiche, followed by an absolutely exquisite filet of charolais beef with *gratin dauphinois*. This was followed by a cheese service that featured my favorite cheese that she had introduced to me – Ami du Chambertin. We shared a nostalgic moment about that, and I felt more and more that they were starting to be impressed with Franck, despite their initial reservations. By the time dessert—a large meringue and chocolate cake from that wonderful patisserie in Nuits-Saint-Georges—was served, Franck had everyone fully under his spell.

Sophie moaned. "How I wish I had a boyfriend too!"

Robert drew his brows together. "You need to concentrate on your studies."

"Laura's doing both!" she protested.

"It's true that Laura is a natural intellectual," Franck said. "She always amazes me at how brilliant she is and how hard she works. I never want to distract her, only support her."

Everyone looked a bit slack-jawed at this proof of wonderful-ness.

"You see!" Sophie said to her parents. "I could do both."

"But Franck is not just any man," said Danielle and smiled

warmly at me.

"It's true," Robert said. "It seems to me like he may be one of the few men who are worthy of our Laura."

And with Antoine still sulking in his seat, just like that, Franck managed to get their vote of approval.

chapter thirteen

I was flying high the next few days, until the day that Stéphanie and I went to Dijon to shop *les soldes,* the after-Christmas sales.

The shopping itself was great fun. Dijon was a stunning town to begin with, and the streets of were still decorated and bustled with shoppers. Steph and I had so many laughs and she told me all about her new classes to become a nurse, the weird stories from the co-ops she'd done so far, as well as all the gossip about our café gang from high school.

Franck was happy to stay back in Villers and hang out with Mémé and the rest of his family. Now that Christmas was over, we were acutely conscious of the days going by too fast. We left on January second and it was almost New Year's.

I couldn't buy much because I had to fit everything in my suitcase, but I did buy a new grapevine bottle opener to take to Montreal with us, as well as a miniature stone statue of Saint-Vincent.

When we burst back into the cozy kitchen at Franck's house, Stéphanie was ahead of me but stopped short, making me run into her back.

"Ouf. What—" I peered past her and saw Juliette, ensconced at the round kitchen table, having afternoon tea with Mémé and Michèle. What was *she* doing there? Where was Franck? A sick feeling of mistrust gripped my body. I hated being thrust into a situation I wanted no part of.

Stéphanie started moving again. We shuffled into the kitchen with our bags and I shut the door behind me.

"Juliette," Stéphanie said, her tone much colder than her usual friendly self. "I haven't seen you in so long.

Franck and Stéphanie had told me that Juliette and Stéphanie used to be friends before Franck and her started going out.

Once Juliette had bagged Franck, she'd started being awful to Steph. Why Franck put up with it, I'd never understand...or maybe the answer was all too obvious. Even sitting in the kitchen on a cold winter day she looked exquisite – blond hair straight and silky down her back, turquoise eyes bright and innocent-looking, highlighted by a pale blue sweater and a slim-cut pair of jeans. Ugh.

"I thought I'd come and have a little visit," Juliette said. "I've been missing all of you so much, you know, after seeing Franck again in Beaune—"

"You saw Franck?" Stéphanie asked her.

"Yes, in Beaune at the *café Baltardises*. We just bumped into each other."

I was there too! I wanted to scream.

"Funny," Steph said. "He didn't mention it to me. I guess he forgot."

Juliette had that brief moment of looking pissed-off before she replaced it with a serene expression. I'd never adored Steph or her staunch loyalty more than in that instant.

"Well, I didn't forget," she said. "He promised he'd come over for a drink, but I hadn't heard from him, so I thought I'd drop by to say hello."

Michèle smiled at Juliette. "And it was very kind of you to do so. It was wonderful to hear how your parents are doing. It's strange that I haven't bumped into them in so long."

Michèle's pleasure at seeing Juliette again made all of those doubts come stampeding back. Of course, she would rather Franck be with Juliette and settle back in Villers, than go back to Québec with me. I could hardly blame her for that.

"Where is Franck?" I interjected.

"He's off somewhere with Olivier and Martial," Juliette answered for Michèle, casting herself in the role of insider.

"How do you know that?" Stéphanie asked Juliette.

"Because I told her," Mémé said, her eyes narrowed in Juliette. Ah, so I had another on my side. My heart warmed at that. "Did you two have a nice time?" Mémé asked us.

"Of course we did!" Stéphanie said. "It's impossible not to have a good time with Laura."

Oh my God I loved her. "It was fantastic," I agreed.

"Well Juliette," Mémé said. "I suppose I should start in on dinner. This was, in no uncertain terms, the signal for Juliette to push off, yet she showed no intention of doing so.

"Oh! I remember how delicious your cooking is Madame Menneveau," Juliette said. Juliette was using the formal *vous* form as well as addressing Franck's grandmother by her formal name rather than Mémé, which is what Mémé told me to call her the first time we met. There had to be something in that.

"Yes, well, I've been making a lot of Laura's favorites on this trip," she said. I smiled at her over Juliette's head.

That annoyed look flashed on Juliette's face again. This cozy kitchen where I had enjoyed so many moments of happiness over the past two weeks now felt like a battleground.

The door opened, and Franck came in, smelling of the icy air and with the scent of apple brandy on his breath. He looked lovely with his wool scarf wrapped around his neck and his winter jacket.

He grinned at me. "*Salut mon amour.*" He swept me up in a kiss, before even turning his gaze to anyone else. "Did you and Steph have fun?"

"We did," I said and then kissed him again. "It looks like you had fun too. Calvados?"

He just smiled and winked at me. Over his shoulder I could see Juliette had stood up in her chair.

"Franck," she tapped his shoulder. "*Bonjour.*"

He turned around, but he still had an arm around my shoulder. "Juliette!" he exclaimed. "I wasn't expecting to see you here." He shot a questioning glance at Steph, who just gave him a resigned shrug back.

She reached up and brushed his arm. A prickly sensation bloomed in my gut. She wasn't his to touch anymore. "I came to check if you'd forgotten all about your promise to me."

Franck frowned. "Promise?" His arm stayed around my shoulders and I tried to focus on that.

"To come to my house for an *apértif.*"

"Oh...right," Franck said. It was obvious to everyone in the kitchen that he'd completely blanked.

"You must go!" Michèle said. "Juliette's parents are surely longing to catch up with you."

Michèle couldn't be blamed for subtlety.

Franck frowned. "Tomorrow night is the only—" Franck began.

"Wonderful!" Juliette beamed. "I'll tell my parents to expect you at six thirty?" She'd gone and used the singular again, and nobody in the room except maybe Michèle and Franck assumed it was a slip of the tongue.

"Laura too, *bien sûr,*" Franck added. Mémé was wringing a dishtowel in her hands within an inch of its life. I rather thought she wished it was Juliette's neck, and I had never felt quite so in tune with Franck's grandmother.

"Right!" There was that peevish expression again, gone almost as quickly as it appeared. "Of course! Laura too."

"Laura," Franck said to me. "We're due over at Martial and Isabelle's for dinner. Remember? We're already late. I came to pick you up."

"Oh, right." I'd been so flustered by Juliette in Franck's kitchen that I had completely forgotten. That was so unlike me.

"How *are* Martial and Isabelle?" Juliette asked, making her way to the door, but far too slowly for my taste. "I miss them too."

Franck tilted his head to one side. "You barely knew them," he said. "And what you knew, you didn't particularly like, if I recall correctly." For once, I was overcome with gratitude that Franck couldn't dissimulate to save his life.

"Oh." She gave a pretty shrug of one shoulder. "You must be mistaken. Anyway, I'll be off, see you tomorrow night!" She'd used the singular again. There was no language as ideally suited to linguistic digs as French.

After she'd left, Franck turned to me. "Are you ready?"

At that moment, there was nothing I wanted as badly as to escape that kitchen. "*On y va.*"

"Why did she show up here?" Stéphanie said, indignant.

"It was lovely," Michèle said, a steely undertone to her voice. "We had a nice catch-up."

"Speak for yourself," Mémé muttered. "I know a homewrecker when I see one."

I understood Michèle's reasoning, but it hurt all the same. The Christmas before Franck had managed to completely win over my family. I was under the illusion that I'd made headway in that direction on this vacation, but now the fact that I hadn't hit me like a slap across the face. I didn't even think my presents left behind in Montreal would have made a whiff of difference.

"Mémé," Michèle said. "Don't be like that. Juliette is a nice village girl, and I went to school with her father. We go way back."

The implication hung in the air…I, on the other hand, was still an unknown entity.

Just then Martial appeared at the kitchen door. "Your chariot awaits!" he announced. "I'll drive you down."

"Awesome." I made haste out the kitchen door into the courtyard, just leaving my bags where I'd dropped them. I needed to escape. "I can't wait."

Martial took a puff of his cigarette and nodded at Franck. "I saw Juliette in the street. That was a blast from the past. What was she doing here?"

"I'm not exactly sure," Franck said. "But she's gone now."

Maybe, but only temporarily.

"Are you sure you want me to come?" I asked Franck the next evening, as he got dressed to go for the *apéritif*. We'd been at his aunt Renée's eating all day with about ten other family members, so I didn't have the chance to talk to him about Juliette, even if I knew how to bring it up, which I didn't.

My mind had been gnarled into a messy tangle since the scene in the kitchen the day before. Our departure was only three days away, so everything was tinged with rising panic and emotion anyway. Somehow, it didn't feel fair for me to create a crisis for Franck at such a juncture. He'd never led Juliette on or excluded me, so...what basis did I have to bring it up?

Still, all night I'd had tortuous dreams of coming downstairs for breakfast to find that Michèle had arranged an impromptu wedding between Franck and Juliette and I arrived in my dressing gown for coffee to find myself in the middle of it.

The dream was an exaggeration, yes, but it wasn't completely out of left field. The day before, Michèle had blatantly encouraged Juliette's interest in Franck, even when I was standing right there. It had been heartening to have Mémé and Stéphanie on my side, but Michèle was Franck's *mother*...that stung.

"Of course," Franck said. "I'm not going there without you."

I didn't respond, but just zipped up my best black pants with the growing heaviness of impending doom.

No matter what clothes I picked, I knew I would feel like a frump beside Juliette. Whatever I chose from the limited selection in my suitcase, it would not be half as elegant as whatever she was wearing. I possessed only clothes suited to the student life in Montréal—jeans, sweaters, and Doc Martins. I didn't even own a pair of heels. Franck always told me he preferred me out of clothes than in them, but that didn't help much when one was dressing to go to an *apértif* with the parents of your boyfriend's ex-girlfriend.

"Juliette's parents are really nice." Franck came over and put his arms around me. I nestled my head in the crook of his neck and took a deep breath of his familiar scent. "It won't be so bad. You'll see."

"Of course," I said, but thought the opposite. Franck truly had no idea.

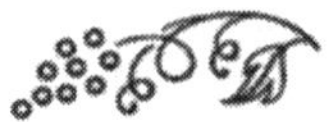

An hour later, my nightmare had sprung to life, which was a relatively rare thing in my experience.

I was sitting on a couch in a room all decorated with burgundy couches and stained wood so dark it looked almost black. The overall effect was oppressive, and it did little to lighten my already grim mood.

I sat on one side of Franck and Juliette had installed herself on the other, as if she was reclaiming her rightful place, if only she could boot me on to the tile floor.

Her parents were perched on an identical couch across from us, their faces wreathed with smiles at having Franck back in their living room again.

Juliette was dressed, as I'd anticipated, in a cocktail dress with strappy high heels, all in her signature color of pale blue. She looked stunning, and I hated her for it.

Juliette was throwing herself into the role of caring spouse, catering to Franck's every thirst or hunger. This meant she was constantly passing him little ovals of baguette spread with pistachio paté and cubes of conté cheese. Franck's forehead was crinkled with confusion, but he remained polite. I would have rather he ask her what the hell she thought she was up to.

The worse thing of all was that Franck was right—Juliette's parents *were* incredibly nice, and not just to Franck.

It was clear they still had a great deal of affection for Franck and missed him in their lives. It was also clear that they felt their daughter had made a mistake when she'd dumped him. However, I also got the impression that they thought, somehow, that Franck was better off with me than their daughter. It was a very odd thing, and not at all what I would have expected, but I kept getting the feeling that they found Juliette almost as annoying as I did.

Juliette's father was asking me about my study program while I sipped my kir. "So, English Literature?" he said. "What made you choose that Laura?"

"I truly love it. I've always adored reading—"

"Laura is also a fantastic writer," Franck interjected.

"It does help to like writing," I admitted. "Most of the evaluation is done through essays, lots and lots and lots of essays."

Juliette's father laughed. "You must go through a lot of pens."

"Oh, I do."

"And you have no interest in French Literature?" Juliette's mother asked. "I always thought if I could go back to *le fac* that's what I would study."

"You never told me that," Juliette said accusingly.

"You never asked," her mother retorted.

"I do actually," I said. "And because McGill is in Montréal, which is a francophone city, it happens to have an excellent French faculty. I'm considering doing a minor in French Literature. I'll have to decide over the next few months."

It was easy to talk to them, and I actually would have enjoyed chatting with them if I wasn't acutely aware of Juliette's toxic presence in the room. In a way, I would have almost preferred it if they'd been irredeemably awful like Juliette. I was starting to see why Michèle was invested in Franck and Juliette possibly getting back together. Juliette's parents were so approachable and friendly. They would, without a doubt, make perfect in-laws.

"Do you think you'd like to go into academia?" Juliette's father asked. "Become a professor, perhaps?"

I considered this, aware of the warm pressure of Franck's fingers intertwined in mine and the reproachful looks Juliette was sending both me and her parents. "That's definitely one route I could take. But I'm not sure I have enough patience for the politics of academia."

"I think Laura should be a writer." Franck squeezed my hand and his eyes shone with undisguised pride.

"I've thought of that," Juliette interjected. "You know, writing a book...I mean, how hard could it be?"

Juliette's parents stared at her with amazement written on their features. "You hated writing in school," her mother said.

"Not to mention reading."

"That's not true." Juliette pouted.

"It is." Her father smiled apologetically. "Remember how annoyed you always were when Franck wanted to read all the time? Of course, people can change, and I believe you're very smart Juliette—I always have, but you were never much of an intellectual like Franck...and Laura," he added, with a smile for me. He seemed to be, unbelievably, on my side.

Juliette made an incoherent sound of outrage. I bit my lip to suppress a smirk.

"Tell me," Juliette's mother injected. "How are your parents Franck?"

"They're doing very well," Franck said. "They send their best wishes, *bien sûr*."

"And your mother's health?"

"She's been very stable, thank you."

"Do give the whole family our love," Juliette's father said.

"I will be sure to do that."

"They told me how difficult they find it with you being so far away." Juliette interjected, leaning towards Franck.

"Well...yes," Franck said, pulling away from her, but she wasn't making it easy.

"Your mother in particular, with her fragile health. I know you would hate the thought of making it any worse by causing her stress."

"Juliette!" Her mother narrowed her eyes at her daughter.

"It's true!" Juliette cried.

Franck patted my knee. "You know what?" I think we should be off. It was lovely to see you both, but we're due for dinner at home.

"Yes, of course," Juliette's father said. He nodded in such a way that convinced me he understood exactly why Franck was making a hasty exit and sympathized completely. "Thank you for coming. It was lovely to see you, and it was a great pleasure meeting you Laura. I have a feeling the two of you will be very happy."

"I think you're right," Franck said. We left, with Juliette fuming in the doorway.

chapter fourteen

I woke up the next morning with a sense of dread covering me like a lead blanket.

We were leaving in two days and the dinner the night before when we returned from Juliette's house had been filled with lamentations about our imminent departure. Michèle had burst into tears and left the table more times than I cared to remember. Mémé kept an embroidered handkerchief clutched in her hand to wipe the corner of her eyes at regular intervals.

This was all my fault. If it wasn't for me and my foreignness, nobody would be in pain, nobody would be crying, and Franck would not have that tension that tightened the corners of his mouth. I had an innate compulsion to make everyone around me feel better, and right now I was faced with complete failure in this task. Worse yet, I was the cause of the problem but saw no solution except breaking up with the man I loved.

I was certain it was not a good time to bring up what Juliette had said about Franck's departure causing his mother's health to go downhill. Knowing Franck as I did, I knew such a possibility would eat away at him. I didn't even know how to approach such a conversation. I was sure my heart would shatter.

It was the morning of New Year's Eve day—a celebration that was traditionally celebrated amongst friends in France. Christmas was with family, and New Year's was with friends. As such, we were having a massive party at Olivier's that served as a New Year's party and a good-bye all at once.

I had been so excited about the party since the start of our trip when Olivier first hatched the idea, yet now our departure, and my guilt around that, cast a pall over everything.

When I got downstairs to the kitchen, Franck was sitting there with his parents and his grandmother. One of his hands was being clutched by Mémé, and Michèle had the other in her grip. Both of them were weeping. Franck sent me a desperate look. Maybe he, too, despite his comfort with emotions of all colors, had reached the breaking point.

"That's right!" he said to me. "We need to go and pick up that thing in Beaune for your mother. How could I have forgotten?"

What thing? I opened my mouth to ask, then I saw the pleading look in Franck's eyes. "Ah yes." I snapped my fingers. "The *herbes de provence*, *fleur de sel*, and all the other things she asked me to bring back for her. Thank God you remembered. I almost forgot."

Franck nodded and stood up, but neither Michèle nor Mémé let go of his hands. "Are you ready to go?" He raised his brows, beseeching.

I wasn't, but I could get ready quick. "Yup. Just need to run upstairs and grab my bag."

When I got back down Franck had disentangled himself, although I had no idea how he'd achieved that feat. Now Michèle and Mémé were clinging to each other, sniffling, while André just watched them, a resigned expression on his placid face.

Franck took the keys off the little wooden antique shelf by the kitchen door. "We'll have Dad's car back by noon."

"I'm making veal's kidneys in calvados for lunch!" Michèle said, with a frown. "Don't be late."

Ah, so that was where the faint smell of urine was coming from. They must have been rinsing the kidneys before I arrived downstairs. I hoped I could just get away with eating some bread and sauce without causing mortal offense, but I would cross that bridge when I got to it. First, I needed to know what was running through Franck's mind, beside immediate escape.

"Remember how Juliette loved my kidneys?" Michèle said as

Franck opened the door out to the courtyard.

Mémé let go of her daughter and scowled at her. "I never liked that girl, and you know it. Stop talking about her."

"Yes," Franck said. "Please do, Maman. I'm with Laura now."

That felt good and bad at the same time. Was I the only reason why he and Juliette hadn't gotten back together? Somehow, I didn't think so, but the past few days were turning me into a mess of doubts in a way I'd never been before.

I had to get out of there. "Let's go," I said, and stepped out into the courtyard. A winter sun hung in the air and a soft light was filtered through the hazy clouds. It felt milder than it had been and even though I rationally knew how far we were from Spring, it felt somehow like it was just around the corner.

Franck grasped my hand and we hurried across the courtyard and into the car. I could tell by the way Franck revved the engine and squealed out of the rue de chaux that he was as eager to get out of there as I was.

When we drove out the gates of Villers-la-Faye, Franck turned to me. "Do you actually need to go to Beaune?"

"No, not really. I picked up all that stuff for my mom last week."

"I just needed to get out of there for a bit." He was driving fast down the dip between Villers-la-Faye and Magny-les-Villers.

I paused for a moment to choose my next words carefully. "Yes, I imagine it all feels a bit...oppressive."

Franck nodded, transfixed by the road ahead. "They just never let up, those two, and they feed off each other."

I chuckled.

"What?" Franck turned to me.

"I just remember Jean made the same observation when he was talking about the scene at Charles de Gaulle when you left the first time."

Franck groaned. "God, how could I forget?"

"So, where do you want to go? "I asked, as we passed the sign at the entrance to Magny-les-Villers.

At the main intersection of the village Franck pulled a sharp right turn that sent me flying against him. Thank God I was wearing my seatbelt.

"I know where to go," Franck said. "I just thought of it now. Sorry, was that turn a little unexpected?"

I chuckled. "You know what? I think I may be getting used to your driving. Now there's a terrifying thought."

Franck let out a bark of laughter and sped up. I understood he knew these roads like the back of his hand, but they were narrow, and everyone drove them like they were in a Formula 1 race.

We burst into the village of Pernand-Vergelesses, the picture-perfect cluster of houses, ancient washing halls, and churches that clung to one of the most scenic hillsides in all of France.

The village was quiet and serene and as Franck turned a sharp right and headed up the hill past an ancient shrine to the Virgin Mary on the right and cascading vineyards to the left, his destination dawned on me.

He was taking me to the statue of Mary at the edge of the field at the precipice of the village. It was where he'd taken me the day after we'd gotten together almost two years before.

I remembered how confused and unsure I'd been. I tried to suppress laughter at the memory, which just resulted in me making a strange choking sound.

"What?" Franck asked. "Are you laughing?"

"Yeah," I admitted.

"Come on, share the joke. I could use a good laugh right now."

"I just remember the first time you took me here," I said. "I wasn't sure if you were going to ravish me or what...I mean, we'd just met."

"*Serieusement?*"

I nodded. "Seriously. I mean, you were almost five years older than me. You seemed so worldly and I felt so awkward, like I had no idea what I was doing."

Franck gave me an affronted look. "I'm only four years older than you."

I shrugged. "Well, like four years and eight months...I'm

rounding up."

"And I thought you were the worldly one. I'd never even been on a plane before, and here you were, living in a different country for a year and planning on going to university in one of the cities I'd daydreamed about as a boy. I felt like a bumpkin."

"But you'd lived in *Paris*."

"And you'd lived in *Canada*...Paris felt very boring in comparison to that."

Franck parked the car and we got out. I took a deep breath of the fresh winter air and could hear some birds—probably the tiny little ones that Michèle fed in her garden all winter—chirping in the distance.

Franck took my hand in his and we made our way across the dew-covered field. I was overwhelmed with déjà vu. "I also thought that a Virgin Mary statue was a rather odd place to take someone on a second date."

"*Vraiment*? But it's beautiful, and the view!"

"I know, but I was just trying to figure it all out...I didn't know you then, and I had no idea who you were or what your intentions were."

The smell of wet soil and grass grounded me to that memory.

"I bet you never anticipated a Christmas Mass at a nunnery." Franck smiled down at me.

"Maybe I should have." We reached the statue, and the spectacular outlook to the sloping valley of vineyards that spooled out in front of us. We both sighed deeply and drank in the view. The pale sun kept peeking out from behind thin clouds, bathing us in light, and then disappearing again.

After several minutes of blessed silence, I sat down on the marble foot of the statue. Mary reigned above me, serene and unperturbable, so unlike myself.

The cold stone soaked through my jeans, but I didn't move. I was overcome with a welcome sensation of feeling anchored for the first time since we'd arrived here in Burgundy. Franck had been right, there was something unique about this spot and somehow I could already feel it was intertwined with our shared identity as a couple.

Could we continue our relationship in Montréal despite his family's reaction to his departure? How long would Franck be willing to make that sacrifice? As things stood now, he had his permanent residency papers for Canada, but I didn't have mine for France. Even if I did, would I be willing to move to France for him as he'd done for me?

"What is it?" Franck sat down and drew me tight against him.

I didn't know how to begin and the last thing I wanted to do was add to his burden. He didn't need to be carrying my emotions on top of everyone else's. "Nothing."

He pulled back enough to be able to study my face. "It's not nothing," he concluded.

"I'm worried about your departure."

"Are you? I'm not."

I sat up then, so I could look him square in the face. What he was saying seemed unbelievable to me. How could he not be panicked at having to make the choice between France and me, yet again? "How can that be?" I asked. "I mean, I saw you when we left your house, how desperate you were to leave in the face of all that sadness—"

Franck shook his head, smiling. "I was running out of things to say to them, that's all. I mean, I realize they have to get it out of their systems, but it does get repetitive after a while."

"But they're going to miss you so much."

"*Oui, c'est sûr.*" Franck caressed my palm with his thumb, making warm, hypnotic circles. "But I know they can handle it. They are adding layer upon layer right now to try and make me feel guilty. That is their technique. I've done this once before, remember."

Now I had started to speak, I couldn't hold the rest of it in. "Your mother is so obviously pushing you back towards Juliette so you'll stay in the village."

Franck shrugged. "Of course. She's just doing that to punish me."

"And me!"

"And you too, yes. But do you know what? She absolutely loathed Juliette when we were together. She's just being contrary, I promise you."

I blinked back tears of relief.

"Wait." Franck took my face in his hands. His touch felt so right against my skin. "You didn't truly think I had the smallest intention of getting back together with Juliette, did you?"

I hesitated. I saw on his face how ludicrous he found the idea.

"Can you blame me? I mean, she's from the village and her parents are really nice people and your family would be so happy—"

"Laura...," Franck leaned down and his lips touched mine with the gentlest, most loving kiss.

"The thing is I can't be anything but myself. I'll never be a village girl like Juliette—"

"I don't want Juliette. I want you." He kissed me again, but I was on a roll.

"I can't make myself smaller or more French for you."

"Thank God for that."

"It's just that, I've been thinking—"

"Sometimes, you just have to put the brakes on that brain of yours." Franck effectively did just that with his coaxing kisses and soothing fingers.

A little while later I was nestled in his arms, finally at peace for the first time in a few days.

"Laura." He stroked my arm. "I need you to listen to me and believe me. I was never truly happy until I found you. I know that in my soul. Juliette was a nightmare, and I only realized how much better a relationship could be when I met you. I can't stand the idea that you have any doubts about my intentions."

I twisted my neck up and pressed my lips against his. The birds chirped in the bushes around us and a rooster was crowing in the distance. "I guess I don't after hearing that."

"Good."

"But I *am* dreading the scene when you leave. I can't help

feeling guilty that it is somehow my fault and that I should be able to make it better."

"Don't think that, truly. Look, my family is dramatic and a bit naughty. They will play this for all it's worth, but you don't need to fix anything—they're not broken, and my mother will be just fine. If they didn't make a scene, then I'd be worried. This visit was fantastic, but there is nothing I want more than for us to go back to Montréal and continue building a life together."

I nodded. "I guess that's it, isn't it?" A new realization dawned on me. "We love our families, and they will always be one of the most important parts of our lives, but the epicenter of it all is us—the two of us—we are the center of our lives now."

"We are each other's family." Franck put it far more succinctly that I had and tightened his arms around me.

"Yes," I said. "I guess we are…well, I guess us and this statue of the Virgin Mary."

"Ah, you're right. How could I forget her?"

epilogue

I had never been so relieved to collapse into my airplane seat as I was on the Air France flight back to Montréal.

The scene at the airport was even worse than anticipated. There was wailing, weeping, and gnashing of the teeth worthy of a biblical tale, but at least Mémé and Michèle didn't end up on the ground again. I decided to count that as a win.

Franck let out a mighty exhale of breath and let his head drop back against his seat. "Thank God that's behind us. They outdid themselves." He reached over and grabbed my hand in his. "Next stop, Montréal." The grin on his face was as sincere as they came.

After our talk at what was becoming "our" spot above Pernand-Vergelesses, the drama had predictably ratcheted up with Franck's family, but there was a new and rock-solid understanding between him and me.

New Year's Eve at Olivier's had been a complete blast, and he was even making noises about maybe venturing on an airplane to come and visit us in Montréal.

Our cabin attendant did his spiel of safety procedures, and afterwards I asked Franck, "Seriously though, how are you feeling? That must have been hard."

"It was," he admitted. "But there had been so many tears in the past few days that I've developed immunity, I think."

"You're going to miss them," I said, not so much a question as a statement of the obvious.

He nodded. "I will, but that is just the way things are for

now. Also, I would bet anything that Mémé is *not* going to die this time either."

"You know," I mused. "I've been thinking more and more about researching that exchange year in Paris next year."

Really?" Franck squeezed my hand. "Do you think it's possible?" The plane backed up and we began to taxi out to the runway.

"I do. I emailed a few people who have done it, and apparently it'll work with my Arts degree and McGill has a ton of exchanges to Paris."

"A whole year back in France," Franck mused. "But not right next door to my family...that sounds perfect."

I leaned back in my seat and indulged in some Parisian daydreaming. It *could* be perfect. Franck would be back in France for a year. His family would be thrilled. Also, come on...a year studying in Paris? It was the stuff fantasies were made of. This was the time in our lives to grab such opportunities, to not play it safe and stick close to the familiar. It sounded like the ideal solution—a gift I could give to both of us.

"I'll make it possible," I said as the plane braked.

Franck blinked, then beamed at me. "I love you."

The engine came to life with a roar. The plane shuddered and began hurtling down the runway for take-off. Our fingers weaved together.

"Here's to the next chapters," Franck said, and made the sign of the cross, as he did when we'd taken off out of Montréal.

Maybe this was a ritual of his. I felt like we'd have many flights together in the future for me to find out.

"Here's to the future." I hoped it would be many more chapters indeed.

La Fin

Sneak peek of Chapter One *My Grape Paris*

My Grape Paris takes fans of Laura Bradbury's Grape Series to the captivating world of Paris, where Laura has managed to organize an exchange year at the Sorbonne. Franck accompanies her, delighted to return to his native France. Over afternoons napping in an ancient Roman amphitheater and nights gallivanting around the Louvre, Laura dreams of becoming a sophisticated Parisian woman.

However, Laura soon discovers that living in Paris is much more complicated than the fantasy. Besides inappropriate relatives and spiteful teachers, there are also questions that become impossible to ignore. Will Franck stay in Paris after Laura's stint at the Sorbonne is up? Is their Parisian year the final hurrah for their romance?

#1 Amazon Bestseller. Hundreds of five star reviews.

chapter one

The only proof I had that I was supposed to be there in Paris was my temporary student visa and a badly photocopied letter from some unidentifiable administrative office of the Sorbonne.

I scanned the letter I clutched in my sweaty hand. It was the last week in August, but the oppressive humidity made it feel as though we were in the tropics—the perfect weather to be sunning ourselves in Biarritz or Brittany, not tramping around the dog poop-festooned streets of the 5th arrondissement of Paris.

What I could decipher from the letter stated that, after my arrival in France, I should contact my exchange year advisor, Professor Alix Renier-Bernadotte, at the address provided. Just an address. No telephone number or any other contact information. *She better be at home.*

We found Professor Renier-Bernadotte's apartment a few streets away from the building where I would be taking at least half of my classes. She lived on a narrow, cobblestoned street, just off a much larger street.

The building rose from the sidewalk in the stately style that was synonymous with Haussmann, the designer of modern Paris—gray stone and large symmetrical windows, fronted by ornate ironwork so Parisians wouldn't tumble out onto the street when opening their massive wooden shutters in the morning.

I was already intimidated by this Parisian professor who was supposed to help me register at the Sorbonne, and I hadn't even met her yet.

Franck and I had arrived that morning after more than fifteen hours of travel from Vancouver. This Inter-University Exchange gig—I was being swapped with a French student who would study for a year at my school, McGill University in Montreal, while I studied at the Sorbonne—was already turning out to be more challenging than it looked on paper.

I studied the name tags stuck in the brass buzzer plate mounted on the wall of the apartment building. They were blurred by age and rain. "Does that look like Renier-Bernadotte to you?" I asked Franck, who was lighting a Gitanes. I didn't know how he could smoke in that heat, let alone Gitanes—the cigarette equivalent of pungent Munster cheese.

He took a deep drag and leaned forward to peer at the name I was pointing at. "It looks to me like it says *Rognon-Betterave.*" Kidney-Beets. He rubbed his stomach thoughtfully. "That gives me an idea. If we find a brasserie, they might have veal kidneys in Madeira on the menu. They're a classic dish at Parisian brasseries, *tu sais.*"

I made a gagging noise.

"You think you don't like them because you've never tried them."

"I know I don't like Gitanes, and I haven't tried them either. I can't get past the smell. Same thing with kidneys."

"Completely different. Kidneys are extremely good for you as well as delicious. Smoking is a filthy habit I need to stop."

"At least we agree on that," I said, then nodded at the buzzers. "So, should I buzz Professor Kidney-Beets here?"

Franck shrugged. "You know my opinion. You should wait until your first day of school. All of Paris goes on vacation in August. Haven't you noticed how empty the streets are?"

"Still—"

"I doubt she's here, and even if she is, she won't answer her buzzer. I warned you not to expect the same welcome that McGill provides to the incoming French students."

That was a shame, because at McGill, the incoming French exchange students were treated like royalty. They were appointed a student chaperone as soon as they arrived in Montreal to help them with everything from finding accommodation to registering for courses to meeting other students.

A whole week of special events were put on for the exchange students freshly arrived at McGill. There were scavenger hunts so they could familiarize themselves with the campus and mingle with others, live concerts, and drinks events so their livers could adapt to Canadian beer and the cheap Czechoslovakian wine from the *dépanneur*. And meetings were set up with various academic advisors so they would have all their questions answered and their timetable completely in order before the beginning of term.

So far, there had been no welcoming committee for me at the Charles de Gaulle airport on our arrival, and the only contact name I had been given was Professor Kidney-Beets, supposedly at this address. As a result, I was pulsing with desperation to connect with her. She was my only shot at feeling less disoriented.

"I have to try," I said. I buzzed on the buzzer.

Nothing.

I buzzed again. Then again.

Franck raised one eyebrow at me. "Does the state of that name tag beside her buzzer look like that of a person who *wants* students to find them?"

Dignified silence was the only possible response to my boyfriend.

I peered up to the two windows on the fourth floor, where Professor Kidney-Beets's apartment was supposed to be if we had indeed chosen the right buzzer. A curtain twitched and a face dominated by a large pair of glasses glanced down, then the curtain drew shut again.

"She's up there!" I shouted in English, even though Franck and I spoke French together most of the time. "I saw her!" I pointed, just in case Franck misunderstood.

I went back and buzzed the buzzer five more times so there could be no doubt I wanted to see her. I was going to buzz it a sixth time, when Franck reached out and stilled my hand. "Ever heard of getting off on the wrong foot? I don't know who this woman is, but I would bet that it's not a prudent idea to piss her off before the school year even begins."

I stamped my foot and buzzed again three times. The curtain above didn't even twitch.

Franck took me by the shoulders and pulled me back from the buzzer. "I'm not sure how it is in Canada, but being so persistent when somebody clearly does not want to answer their buzzer is considered rude in Paris," he said gently.

"I'm not the one who is supposed to be advising students and then hiding away in my apartment, leaving them completely abandoned on the street, not knowing what to do or how to choose their courses or—"

Tears began to roll down my cheeks. Tears borne of too much travel and too little sleep, and overheating and frustration, and the fact that the reality of this whole year-in-Paris thing was already at loggerheads with my fantasies.

"Come on." Franck took my arm. "Let's go find a brasserie."

"I'm not eating kidneys! I won't!" I heard myself shout like a spoiled, overtired toddler.

"You don't have to," Franck said, stroking the back of my hand. "You're to rest your feet for a while, and there might even be chocolate mousse on the menu for dessert."

"We don't have any money," I wailed. "You're always telling me how everything is so expensive in Paris."

"Not the *prix fixe* menu at Paris brasseries. They're a bargain. Besides, a good meal raises one's spirits. That's priceless."

I let myself be led up the street, the hope of meeting Professor Renier-Bernadotte abandoned—for that day anyway.

"Just so you know," I said, "I'll be ordering a carafe of chilled rosé."

"So young, yet so wise." Franck patted my shoulder.

the grapevine

Interested in receiving Laura's French recipes, sneak peeks at her new work, as well as exclusive contests and giveaways, plus countless other goodies?
Sign up for Laura's Grapevine newsletter.

http://bit.ly/LauraBradburyNewsletter

about **Laura**

Bestselling author Laura Bradbury published her first book—a heartfelt memoir about her leap away from a prestigious legal career in London to live in a tiny French village with her Burgundian husband in *My Grape Escape*—after being diagnosed with PSC, a rare autoimmune bile duct/liver disease. Since then, Laura has received a lifesaving living donor liver transplant from her friend Nyssa, published many more Grape Series books and the long-anticipated cookbook to accompany her memoirs, entitled *Bisous & Brioche*. She has also written *The Winemakers Trilogy,* romantic novels set in the Burgundy vineyards, and with renewed health, writes with even more passion than ever.

Now living and writing on the West Coast of Canada with a new liver and three Franco-Canuck daughters (collectively known as "the Bevy"), Laura runs three charming vacation rentals in Burgundy with her husband, has an enviable collection of beach glass, and does all she can to support PSC and organ donation awareness and research.

find **Laura** online

The Grapevine Newsletter
laurabradbury.com/newsletter

Facebook
facebook.com/AuthorLauraBradbury

Twitter
twitter.com/Author_LB

Instagram
instagram.com/laurabradburywriter

Pinterest
pinterest.ca/bradburywriter

BookBub
bookbub.com/authors/laura-bradbury

Books by Laura Bradbury

The Winemakers Trilogy
A Vineyard for Two
Love in the Vineyards

Grape Series
My Grape Year
My Grape Québec
My Grape Paris
My Grape Wedding
My Grape Escape
My Grape Village
My Grape Cellar

Other Writings:
Philosophy of Preschoolers

Laura Bradbury and Rebecca Wellman
Bisous & Brioche

Made in the USA
Las Vegas, NV
08 March 2021

19182929R00090